VOICES OF NEWCOMERS

EXPERIENCES OF MULTILINGUAL LEARNERS

DENISE AMMERAAL FURLONG, ED.D

Published by EduMatch®
PO Box 150324, Alexandria, VA 22315
www.edumatchpublishing.com

These books are available at special discounts when purchased in quantities of 10 or more for use as premiums, promotions fundraising, and educational use. For inquiries and details, contact the publisher: sarah@edumatch.org.

ISBN: 978-1-953852-53-3

CONTENTS

For Tim Furlong,
Ryan Furlong
Joey Furlong
Sarah Furlong

ACKNOWLEDGMENTS

*I would like to thank our students and their families for sharing their stories. I admire them and I learn from them every day. Their voices are powerful and have a positive impact on the world.

*In memory of O: You are remembered and celebrated, even to this day.

*Thank you, Sarah Szamreta Tang, for being my voice of reason and my sounding board. You really are my academic soul mate, in addition to being someone I just think is amazing.

*Thank you to all of the teachers who stepped outside their comfort zone to share their experiences with me. Your stories are important and help amplify the voices of your students. Through your generosity, other teachers will connect with their students by reading about your experiences.

*Thank you to my focus group members: Sarah, Jill, Trish, Carly, and Sharon. I so appreciate your feedback and encouragement and I thank you for keeping me on track. You ladies are all rock stars and I'm humbled that you're on my team.

*Thank you, Lynette & Chris, for being so generous with your time and being my first readers.

*Thank you, Margee Kane Forgosh, for so generously sharing your incredible talent and your beautiful cover design.

*Thank you to my parents in heaven, Bob and Roseann Ammeraal. You always believed in me and I still hope to make you proud.

*Thank you to Sandie, Bobby, Theresa, and Beth for your support. Also, I'm so thankful for my extended family who has kept us afloat in difficult times and celebrated the happy times with us. May we always receive those signs from heaven with joy, knowing that we are always together and will always have that bond.

*Ryan, Joey & Sarah: Thank you for being patient with Mom as she typed away--at night, on vacation, at practice--and pretending to be interested in what I was writing! I'm proud of you all and I can't wait to see what your futures bring. Dream big--but stay close to each other (and your mom and dad!).

*Tim: Thank you for always supporting my crazy dreams and ideas. I love you and I'm so grateful to have you as my partner for life. What a lucky day it was for me when we went to the "Riviera." May we have many more adventures over the years to come!

INTRODUCTION

When children first come to this country, there are many layers to their experience. For some, the travel to their destination may be smooth; for others, it may have been terrifying. The reasons for their move to a new country vary greatly as well. They may know someone in their new destination, or maybe they don't know a soul. Often families have to wait several weeks while they get clearance to attend school—possibly after traveling for an extended amount of time. This can be either a period of gentle transition before beginning school or a time filled with anxiety and strife.

Within the school setting, these students are called "Newcomers" if they have been in our country for a short amount of time before beginning in a given school district. Every Newcomer has his/her own story and has his/her own needs. The following highlights characteristics that may or may not describe your students, but they are important to consider as we strive to teach with **Representative and Connective Pedagogy** (inspired by Culturally Responsive Pedagogy, Ladson-Billings, 1995) in mind.

Some Newcomers...
may be highly educated, and others may have limited or interrupted time in school.
arrived under positive circumstances, and others have undergone horrors that we cannot even understand.
have had exposure to English, and others have never even heard another language.
share their native language with peers in their new country, and others have no one who can communicate with them.
are confident with their literacy skills in their primary language, and others may feel lost when people expect them to know how to read.
are excited and happy to start anew, and others are devastated about leaving home.
are comfortable financially in their new country, and others are struggling for necessities.
have parents who were doctors or professors in their old country, and others' parents had very limited education.
are gifted academically, and others have learning difficulties.
speak a language that shares an alphabet or common sounds/cognates with English, and others have no commonalities between English and their primary language.
have stress and anxiety about their immigration status, and others do not.
left behind close family members, and others' families are intact and together.
have families who very much value school and support education, and others are so overwhelmed with other priorities that it *may appear* that education is not a priority.

The following are characteristics that describe every Newcomer and are also very important to keep in mind as we create those connections and teach respectfully.

ALL Newcomers want to feel accepted and find a niche in the school and community.
ALL Newcomers want to feel safe.
ALL Newcomers deserve an education.
ALL Newcomers make a positive contribution to their new school and community.
ALL Newcomers have a purpose.
ALL Newcomers can learn and have learned throughout their lives.
ALL Newcomers want a nice life.
ALL families want what is best for their children.

This is where the community of the school comes in; we have to acknowledge the gifts and talents that Newcomers bring as well as identify what WE can do for THEM.

Gone are the days in which multilingual learners (MLs) sit in the back of the content-area classroom with work provided by the ESL (English as a Second Language) teacher. Perhaps the teachers didn't even know the language proficiency of their students. No more. **Exactly whose students are they?** There was a time in the past in which classroom or content-area teachers left the education of these students to other people. These students attended their classes but were "kept busy" by assignments from their ESL teachers. Although we sometimes struggle with how to communicate or work with these students, *they belong to all of us.* They come from a variety of different backgrounds and situations, but they all need our support, patience, and attention. **These students become vital members of our classes, our school community, and our towns.** These students are integral parts of our classroom, our school, our district, and our community. They belong and their contribution is valuable.

The goal is to provide equity for these students—it is their **right** to have accessibility to the curricula of the general education students. What this looks like may vary as we provide supports and scaffolds appropriate to their background knowledge and language proficiency, but we never "lessen" our expectations for them or "lower" our goals. Higher-level thinking may look different if students are working on learning content and acquiring language simultaneously.

Let's just make the statement that educators want what is best for ALL of our students, including diverse learners. Many teachers I have met would love to engage these students in their classes but simply do not know how to do so. Some teachers do not understand WHY these students are here and why they should work to meet their needs. This book is meant to be a practical guide to maximizing the learning experience that educators provide for our MLs, Newcomers, and SLIFE (Students with Limited or Interrupted Formal Education). It includes what to do immediately for these students and how to help them progress, both academically and with language acquisition. Things to remember when working with them are discussed. Strategies and techniques to get them engaged are included. Most importantly, the experiences and perspectives of these children are highlighted so we can understand them and support them.

This book is meant to spark conversation and inspire creativity in working with MLs. There are discussion questions for each chapter that are designed to help us connect with the material and with our students. Our passion for teaching does not only include certain "flavors" of students; it must be extended to include children with a variety of backgrounds, SocioEconomic Status, languages, abilities, and cultures. Quotes from students, teachers, and parents are included to provide context to the content of each chapter. If the quotes were translated from another language, it is indicated. Amplifying the Voice (with an intentional capital letter) of these groups in order to better understand their unique stories is the purpose of this book. Please note the use of the singular form of "they/them" throughout this book is used to be inclusive of all students, families, and teachers.

I hope as we read and discuss these perspectives that our relationships and understanding of these groups will allow us to better meet their needs. It is every teacher's responsibility to educate all students in their classes; some just need some support in how best to do so.

1

WHAT ARE THE ABCS OF MLS?

In order to learn new concepts, it's crucial to understand the ways that the lexicon and language are utilized. It is then that we can accept ownership of understanding those concepts, as well as increase our knowledge through communication with others.

Reflection questions:

- Is there a sport or activity that you really don't enjoy watching or participating in because you don't understand the rules or the terminology?
- Compare your classroom experiences as a teacher (or preservice teacher) with those you had as a student. Were there things that you didn't realize were happening in the classroom as a student that you now understand? Are there things that you learned as a teacher that you would do differently than you experienced as a student?

"I got off the bus and cried. I didn't know nothing--the language, where to go, what to do. No one spoke my language. Then a teacher came to me and smiled."

Language of Educating Multilingual Learners

There are many different ways that educators describe things that apply to our second language learners. These acronyms can get confusing, but they are crucial to understand so we are all speaking the same language. Following are some descriptions of the language used when discussing these learners and the ways we provide their education.

ELLs/ELs, DLLs, MLLs/MLs, and ESL

Years ago, we used to refer to all students who come to our schools as "**ESL** kids" (or in my district, "Spanish students"—whether or not they actually spoke Spanish), which stands for English as a Second Language. Variations of this could include ESOL (English to Speakers of Other Languages), ENL (English as a New Language), or maybe EAL (English as an Additional Language) to cover students for whom English may be part of a multilingual skills set. ***"Miss, I already speak two languages, so I don't need English as a Second Language. It's my third!"***— translated and laughing. Now, ESL is more commonly referred to as a class or a program in districts rather than referring to a label for the children who are serviced. And, as an aside, "Spanish students" would refer to students who take Spanish as a World Language class (or students who happen to be from Spain), rather than the language some students speak natively.

MLLs or **MLs** (multilingual learners) are what many people currently call students who are speakers of other languages who are learning English. Most recently, people have used **ELLs** (English language learners) or **ELs** (English learners), but there has been a shift to highlight the strengths of these multilingual children rather than a focus solely on learning English. These students were also formerly known as LEP (Limited English Proficient) students, and the change in terminology came as we saw these children through an asset-based lens rather than focusing on what they "lack." We want to be sure that the language acquisition process is an "additive" process (rather than "subtractive") that enriches their lives rather than takes away their native language and literacy. Many people focus on a "growth mindset" when working with children and adults alike, and acknowledging the positive parts of learning another language (rather than limited proficiency) definitely falls in this category.

The recent move towards the more inclusive term "ML" reflects the diverse linguistic backgrounds that these students have. Not only does this honor their native or dominant languages, but it acknowledges that they are still learning and growing in those languages (as one does throughout life) while they add English to their repertoire. Powerful language is needed such as this to frame this type of mindset about our students and their languages.

Multilingual learners sometimes come to our schools with many more academic exceptionalities than learning language. Although their "classification" solely mentions their language differences, these students may—or may not—require other types of assistance or attention from their teachers. This attention may come in the form of advanced classes in mathematics or science or intervention services in other areas in which they may struggle. Instruction for MLs should be as individual as they are. But it must be noted that English services are NOT interventions; they are strategically targeted language supports that facilitate language acquisition in the four domains of language (speaking, listening, reading, writing). There is nothing "remedial" about this.

DLLs are Dual Language Learners who are MLs age six or younger. These students are learning English simultaneously as their native language, both in terms of oral language and literacy. This distinction is important to recognize because they are still developing language and literacy in their first language and hopefully will do so simultaneously with acquiring English. DLLs may certainly need some accessibility modifications to acquire English, but their native-language peers are also learning the fundamentals of English and literacy alongside our DLLs. To be clear, I feel strongly that all students are language learners, even when learning in their dominant language at an older age. However, this designation refers to the development of literacy, language, and the pragmatics that go along with two languages at the same time alongside one's peers at the primary level.

There are many different types of supports we can provide for our MLs, with **ESL class** being one of them. Depending upon the language proficiency level of our students, ESL support can look very different in different settings, but two things remain the same: a certified, highly-qualified passionate advocate who knows the needs of his/her population is the ESL teacher, AND the general education must be knowledgeable about their needs and willing to do whatever possible to help these students succeed.

POEs/SIFE/SLIFE

Some Newcomers come to us with solid and consistent foundations in education and others do not. Those who do not are considered to be **SLIFE** (sometimes referred to as **SIFE**), who are Students with Limited or Interrupted Formal Education. By classification (in some states), SLIFE have missed 2+ years of education in their native country (or the country in which they lived while of educational age) or are 2+ years behind in academic levels where they should be according to their age. This can happen for a variety of reasons, all of which have a clear and visible effect on these children. They may have experienced trauma or loss in their lives, during which school may not have been the priority or their struggles absolutely inhibited their attendance. They may have not been able to attend school because of financial reasons. Some do not go to school because of fear of gangs, police, or perhaps abuse. For some, moving house took an extended amount of time, whether it was within their country or when they immigrated to the United States. For just about all of them, there are difficulties for them to overcome because of their educational experiences.

We have to be clear to understand that each Newcomer (and each student, for that matter) has his or her own story and no strategy is "one size fits all." We heard that one of our Newcomers had come to us via Texas after Hurricane Harvey wreaked havoc there. What we found out later is that she never really lived there outside of a brief stop at a center for immigrants. She came initially from Honduras, but also spent time in Tokyo and became fluent in Japanese before returning home to Honduras. Her intelligence and educational experience helped her immensely in school and in her acquisition of English. Not only did she exit our ESL program within two years, but we recommended her for the Gifted & Talented program the following year. A different Newcomer who came that same year in our 8th grade had very little literacy in his native language and only attended school in his home country until 1st grade. Not only were academics very difficult for this student, but also the norms and rules of the school. Many students fall somewhere in between, and we have to assess all students' needs and meet them where they are, academically, emotionally, linguistically, and socially.

EBs/DBs

Emergent Bilingual (**EB**) is another term for people who are acquiring a second language. Sometimes this is used synonymously with "Newcomer," but EBs can also include children who were born in the United States but not exposed to English until they attend school. EBs, or **DBs** (Developing Bilinguals), do not have to be new to the country, but they are new to the language. The term "Emergent Bilingual," much like "Emergent Literacy" in the world of reading, refers to someone at the beginning of the process yet with the potential to achieve success. To be clear, this "success" is not just proficiency in the target language; proficiency and literacy in both languages are key. Again, this is a positive perspective in terms of the eventual "end goal" of bilingualism, rather than focusing on the proficiency that they have not gained yet.

Another way to view the language acquisition of these students may include examining the order in which they acquire languages. Simultaneous Bilinguals are children who were exposed to two languages in the home before the age of three, with the assumption that they are acquiring both languages at the same time. Sequential Bilinguals include children who began acquisition of their second language later, perhaps as they start school. This information is really just to give context about how and when these students acquired language and may not have any effect on their later proficiency in either language.

L1/SLA/BICS/CALP

Second Language Acquisition (**SLA**) is the means through which our students are gaining another language. Our students can either "acquire" or "learn" a language and, believe it or not, there is a huge difference between the two (Krashen & Terrell, 1983). Learning a language requires one to memorize tenses and vocabulary and really not use the language in context. People who learn a language are the ones who get good grades in high school Spanish but later report that they still cannot speak or understand the language after four years of study. If the focus is on "learning a language" (rather than acquiring), success may be measured in terms of good quiz grades rather than communicative use of the language. One does not gain access to language through memorization, but rather by experiencing and learning through the language.

According to Sociocultural Theory (based on the work of Vygotsky, 1978), acquiring a language is something completely different. If people focus on acquiring language through interactions with others, the results are much more effective. These language producing opportunities are authentic and provide all students with the chance to interact with peers in the target language. Not only are these students acquiring language, but they are also forming relationships with peers. Teachers with a communicative focus provide opportunities for students to use and understand language at a level appropriate for their language proficiency.

When discussing SLA, **L1** is the term used to refer to the learner's primary or dominant language. This may or may not be the first language that was spoken by the learner, but it is the one they know best and can possibly leverage knowledge of this language to acquire other languages. Teachers must exercise extreme caution when limiting students' use of their L1 (*"English only, please!"*), as no one would like to send the message to students that their L1 is not valued or useful. As our dominant language is part of our self-identity, this can be detrimental to the students' self-esteem. Also important to note is the fact that some Simultaneous Bilinguals may not have a dominant language, as they acquired more than one language at the same time; being respectful of their unique language repertoires as well is essential.

BICS (Basic Interpersonal Communicative Skills) and **CALP** (Cognitive Academic Language Proficiency) are types of language acquisition described by Cummins (2000). BICS is the more "surface" language acquisition of social and basic language; this develops first and can develop over 1-2 years. CALP is the academic language that students need to succeed in content-area classes; this could take 5-7 years or more. A more recent webinar by Cummins (2020) indicated that it is important to note here that there is no "time limit" for language acquisition. Whether or not there are other underlying challenges, it is perfectly reasonable for lifelong language learners to still be acquiring language, even if it's well past the time that has been recommended. We must remember how complex languages are and that people acquire them at different rates.

Many people who are not familiar with these phases of language acquisition may be fooled when they hear students who have mastered language at the BICS level. These students appear to have become fluent in English, as they have the ability to speak well in social situations or can answer questions fluidly. However, they may still struggle in the more complex parts of language acquisition, especially in academic areas, which is more at the CALP level. It is at this level of language that many of our students need the most support.

Another challenge when it comes to this type of language proficiency is the possibility that the learner did not achieve CALP in their native language. This means that there will be little transfer of knowledge while learning these complex language facets and leveraging native language will not be as effective in these situations. We often see this with our students with interrupted education or those whose school systems in their native country are very different from those in the new country.

SEI, COLOs

Sheltered English Instruction (**SEI**) is a protocol in which educators teach content through a lens of language acquisition. MLs attend grade-level content-area classes with teachers who are either ESL teachers or general education teachers who are trained in SEI. This protocol focuses on providing **accessibility** to content areas for MLs through strategies that engage them at the level at which their language allows them to participate and gain that content knowledge while acquiring English.

There are content objectives and language objectives (**COLOs**) for each class, and teachers use a variety of techniques that benefit all students but specifically help to build language proficiency while teaching content. For instance, the content objective deals with the concepts associated with science or social studies, while the language objectives refer to the types of language output that would be measured in this lesson. As all students are learning literacy and language through the content areas, COLOs are useful for classes of students at all levels.

For teachers who are just beginning to use Sheltered English strategies, COLOs are quite a challenge and often met with some resistance. It is sometimes viewed as "extra work" or more on the plates of already exhausted teachers. However, it's important to be intentional with both content and language objectives for all students as this keeps the teacher cognizant about providing opportunities for students to measure progress in both.

F1, F2

Our goal as ESL teachers is to get our students to the point that our students are determined that they do not need ESL services any longer. But these students cannot be completely off our radar yet. Once learners are "exited" (or graduated) from ESL services, they are still entitled to monitoring or assistance from an ESL teacher for two years. F1 (Former year 1) and F2 (Former year 2) are ways to denote that these students are still under the umbrella of ESL services, even though they've gained enough language proficiency to exit the program.

Unfortunately, there is sometimes a gap between demonstrated proficiency on standardized tests and success and confidence in general education classes without language supports in place. Exiting from ESL services must be viewed from a "multiple measures" perspective. One must consider—in addition to the ACCESS or other standardized testing—the child's literacy level, success in content-area classes, and dependence upon accessibility modifications. Social and emotional factors must be considered as well. Educators don't want these learners to "fall off the cliff" of supports, so this type of monitoring is considered to be part of a step-down process designed to help students succeed.

UIC/UMs

Unaccompanied Immigrant Children (**UIC**) or Unaccompanied Minors (**UMs**) are children who cross over the border into the United States alone. Some of these children are coming to their parents or family who are already living in the United States; others are not. Either way, this journey for these children is not one that is often made under the best of circumstances.

In Chapter 9, we discuss the story of O., a child who came into the United States with his sister to live with his father who had lived here for years. O. and his sister hadn't seen their father in several years and were now essentially leaving the family they knew to go to live with a stranger. This is what some of our UMs experience with all of those accompanying emotions.

Other children come into the United States without a parent or family member waiting for them. These children may be fleeing a dangerous or traumatic situation and really are entering a new country without a safe harbor to welcome them. Once they are attending school, this may be a place in which they have continuity and safety.

What teachers need to know about all of these students is that they have been through experiences that most certainly have made an imprint on their emotional health. Like all of our students, each of these children is unique and no one strategy will fit all of their needs. Also refraining from judging anyone's experiences (or feeling "sorry for them!") is absolutely necessary.

Reflection discussion:

Reflection 1: People who "understand the rules" (or norms?) feel ownership or kinship with others who also have this understanding. Those who are football (or hockey or lacrosse…) fans share this common language and shared experiences. People connect with one another while discussing the intricacies of the game. If Bob is at the sports bar during the World Cup and he doesn't have interest or knowledge of soccer, he is left out of the experience and may even have little interest in talking with anyone. If Bob is there without his friends but knows the language and details of the game, he is able to interact with others based on this connection alone.

When our MLs understand the way the school runs, as well as a working knowledge of the basic language needed, they feel as if they have belonging or ownership in this community. Without explicitly learning the norms or rules of the class or school, the MLs may choose to "opt out" like Bob did when he didn't understand soccer. If Marguerite feels comfortable that she knows when she should raise her hand to leave the room or understands when her next opportunity to eat is during the day, she may feel more apt to take risks in learning the language. Because she understands and feels competent in the basic norms of the classroom, she is willing to take those risks on the next level: learning content and using language.

Similarly, some teachers feel less confident about educating MLs. These teachers may be veteran teachers of different populations, but at a loss when given the (rewarding) challenge of Newcomers or SLIFE in their classes. It seems that everything they've ever learned about teaching is challenged by these students. But, if they are open to learning more about SLIFE and Newcomers, their perspectives of teaching will widen and their abilities to meet the diverse needs of all of their students will increase. The more they learn about these students and their assets, the more they will enjoy and feel more confident in their abilities to educate them.

Reflection 2: Many teachers say, "Everyone thinks they are an expert at teaching, just because they were students for 12 years!" It's true that after doing something for several years, one tends to understand it well. However, there are so many "behind-the-scenes" strategies and split-second decisions in teaching, that it's impossible for a casual observer to understand all that takes place.

Novice teachers often focus on content-area facts and classroom management in order to survive their first months. As they become more comfortable in their classroom and confident in their ability to teach, these teachers often focus on parts of teaching that are more nuanced and even try some things that a more seasoned teacher takes for granted. It is the same with MLs; once they get past survival, they then attempt using the language in more and more situations.

Using our past experiences as a student can very well affect how we teach. We remember how we felt as students, both positively and negatively, and the role of the teacher in those situations. We build on connections to past experiences to assess new situations. Conversely, our Newcomers may have educational experiences that are so different from ours that they have trouble connecting what they know about school to their current placement. Helping these students build schema and background in varied experiences in school will help them adjust as they change classes or placements in the future.

In both of these situations, it's about putting oneself in the situation of our students. Teachers may sometimes let their frustration in getting a new student who doesn't speak English be in the way of really being empathetic and responsive to a child's needs. Educators have the opportunity to be the advocate that a Newcomer sorely needs. Take the opportunity and embrace it. You, teachers, make the difference!

2

BACKPACK OF EXPERIENCES

People often think their own experiences, background or traditions are the "right" ones, without ever considering the beauty in diversity.

Reflection questions:

- What are some cultural norms from your own culture or family that others may think are "strange?"
- What five "categories" would you use when describing yourself? How do you think the following Newcomer would describe himself?

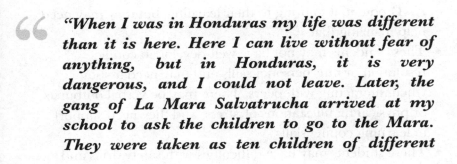

> ***"When I was in Honduras my life was different than it is here. Here I can live without fear of anything, but in Honduras, it is very dangerous, and I could not leave. Later, the gang of La Mara Salvatrucha arrived at my school to ask the children to go to the Mara. They were taken as ten children of different***

grades. They returned more often to the school where I was. The teachers and the director tried not to let them pass, but the men of the Mara bothered and threatened. The next day the administration let them go to school. La Mara went to my class to watch and take notes from the students to recruit them into the gang. Then they left, but they waited outside the school until we left. They saw me and called me to them and told me I had to do them favors. I told them, "no," the members threatened me with my family and with much fear I told them yes, and for a few months I did what they want."

What do teachers need to know for students who may have had experiences such as these?

- These students may have interrupted education (either through time that they missed or from stress) and may not have solid academic skills in their native language. This can definitely have an impact on one's SEMH (Social Emotional Mental Health), as stress associated with perceptions of academic and linguistic "inadequacy" can be overwhelming. To be clear, these students have a wealth of life experiences AND potential to bring to their learning, but they may need help realizing that.
- These students may not have well-developed conflict resolution or interpersonal skills and may need assistance when interacting with peers. There may be verbal outbursts or physical manifestations of stress, and they need support in learning coping skills.
- These students may have difficulties with safety drills and

assemblies that may bring up memories of their past (or present?) fears. Explicit instructions in their dominant languages to ensure they understand that they are not in danger is critical, as well as discussing these drills before they happen. During these first drills, a peer buddy can be a resource to help these students know what to do, as well as helping them keep calm.

- If counseling services are available in the school (in their native language?), these students would benefit. If not, there may be community resources that the school can help their families secure SEMH assistance.
- Educators must watch for possible gang involvement or aggressive language or actions and help form a plan to support these students. We must acknowledge that this type of involvement does not indicate that this child is "bad" or has violent tendencies. There are many reasons why some children may gravitate towards gangs, including a sense of belonging or monetary reasons. If they get support from other sources, they may not go this route. Mentoring programs at school can help provide students with an outlet for asking questions and fostering positive connections with peers and adults.
- Some students want to talk about their past experiences and others do not. Respect them either way. They do not owe anyone their story.
- These students' families may or may not be together, and these students may have worries about their family left behind. Be sensitive when doing projects that involve information about families (family trees, investigations into one's family roots).
- Educators are not here to "save" students like these; rather we are just here to help and support them as much as we can through this part of their life.
- As these students learn English, they will be multilingual or

bilingual young adults. With this in mind, a growth mindset with an asset-based perspective is key to fostering success for them. We must not focus on what they cannot do at this point, but rather what their goals are and how we will help them achieve those goals and beyond.

- These students have great love and loyalty for their families, and they have people who love them as well. We are not to judge any decisions that ANY family makes, but support their children to the best of our abilities.
- These students want to feel wanted and accepted. We must make it a point to provide them with opportunities to make connections with other students and adults. It is through those connections that they will feel a sense of belonging.
- There is more to any student than we see in the classroom—acknowledging the "life" that children have outside the school is key to validating their journey.
- These students have the potential to make amazing contributions during their lives...and they will!

New child on the class list...

Some teachers view the arrival of Newcomers with a groan and annoyance. "How am I going to help them? Are they even going to know any English? These kids just doubled my workload! How does the admin expect me to teach these kids? I don't have room for any more students!" Newcomers are sometimes viewed as a burden, rather than an **opportunity to be an agent of change** for the lives of the entire class. Students such as these students may (or may not!) present difficulties in class because of past trauma and experiences, but are very much in need of the support of teachers and school community.

When a new name shows up on the class list, the teacher must determine what the immediate needs of the student are and how to best make them feel at home in the classroom. This is not a "savior" crusade; it's the job of the teacher, no matter the situation of the student. We can compare this to the triage nurse in a hospital: We evaluate and determine the level of support that each child needs at that time, and we coordinate the team effort to meet the child's needs. As they settle in with us, the needs may change, and we should be flexible with those changes.

Every child brings a "backpack" of experiences, both positive and challenging, to new situations. This backpack colors everything that the child feels or accomplishes. In these backpacks, our students carry their academic schema, emotions, values, beliefs, and memories. These backpacks can also provide our classrooms with a rich diversity of contributions from all of the students.

A child's backpack may include school experiences, life experiences, travel to or from faraway places, language or cultural diversity, and many more things that will certainly enrich whichever class the child joins. This backpack may also include loss, trauma, missed education, anxiety, uncertainty about their place in life, among other things. But it's important to understand that each child is more than what is in their backpack, especially if the challenging things are more visible at first. It's the teacher's responsibility to provide enrichment for the student in these cases and make the classroom as welcoming and supportive as possible.

First things first

There are many variables to consider in terms of placement of Newcomers within a district, and they are sometimes considered to be controversial. But educators must consider these variables, especially ones that may not be immediately visible upon arrival. Multilingual learners are more than language differences, and SLIFE are more than missed education (or the gaps that may exist there).

Every Student Succeeds Act (ESSA) provides for consistency for the protocol when a Newcomer first arrives in a school district, at least at the state level (Garcia Mathewson, 2016). Certain procedures—such as identifying and testing potential MLs—are required to be met for all students who enter a school district to ensure all children get the services to which they are entitled.

Often students' arrivals at our schools may predate the arrival of their school records. The first experience that children and their families have at our school is crucial for how they will feel about being there. So, ensure that office staff are friendly and patient, and —even when just dropping off papers—students and their families are greeted by the ESL contact, administration, the nurse, or whoever else can help make this a positive and supportive experience. We have seen office staff very short-tempered with new families in terms of not having the correct paperwork or coming at inconvenient times, and this can cause anxiety for the children and their families before they even begin school. Although we cannot predict the future and may not know every language of every student before they enroll, it is important to have the information needed for these families available in as many languages as there are in the community. This cannot be stressed enough: Newcomers and their families must feel safe and supported in this new environment, and that starts from the first contact.

At this point, we place students who are new to the country appropriately in terms of their ages and then determine which services they may require. The Home Language Survey completed by their parents or guardians gives a sense of where to begin. Rather than being part of a checklist, the HLS can be immensely valuable in terms of beginning communication with our Newcomers' families.

Screening for ESL services must take place immediately or before the new students begin, as it may affect their placements and daily schedules. If ESL services are necessary, the ESL teacher should be the point person for all needs of these students. It is essential that the ESL support is appropriate for each student's level of English acquisition and support needed in the content area classes.

Also, knowledge of former schooling is critical, but students should be placed age-appropriately even if they have not attended schooling consistently up to that point. This is sometimes debated because many educators want to place students where they feel they can educationally meet their needs, but it is crucial for several reasons:

Grades or levels: Grades may not be similar in other countries to our system in the United States—and this statement can be interpreted in different ways. For one thing, it may be apples and oranges if we make comparisons between fourth grade in different countries. There may be different skills or curricula associated with grade levels in other countries, so one cannot assume that students who have completed school up until the grade previous to current age-appropriate placement have similar educational experiences to their peers. Grades students earn may have different values in other countries as well. It may be a challenge to see how success was evaluated in students' former countries, even with access to report cards.

Peers: It is important to keep students with their same-aged peers as much as possible. A student may have academic skills only up to second grade but is the age of 8th graders. What would it do to the social-emotional health of a teenager to be placed with much younger kids, even though academically they may be at similar levels? I agree that it is difficult for older students to be placed where they academically cannot find success yet, but it is important to build in the academic support in an environment in which students are appropriately placed. It is the responsibility of the district to meet students' needs and *not the fault of the students* if they do not have the skills one may expect from students of that age. It is also important to note what children experience in terms of the physical and emotional changes that come with puberty and how crucial it is to be with same-aged peers during this time.

Curricula: Access to grade-level curricula is the right of all students. While there may have to be modifications and scaffolding made in terms of accessibility, students must have the opportunity to learn what their peers are learning. Although a student's academic level may be more on par with a much younger student, we must teach with dignity in mind. A teenager should not be taught with materials appropriate for first grade. Period.

Graduation rates: Schools must keep in mind the age at which students can legally quit school (as pessimistic as it is to discuss). Students who are not kept with students close to their age may be more likely to quit school as soon as they are able. Students must be placed close to their peers and given as much support as they need to progress. It is through this support that schools engage and empower students to set and keep these academic goals.

It should also be noted that MLs should not be excluded from upper-level content area classes (or Gifted/Talented classification) because of their developing language. Although it may be difficult for Newcomers to be assessed for placement in classes, placements for MLs must be made with potential in mind. To be clear, scheduling challenges do NOT affect a student's potential to participate in Enrichment or Gifted classes; it is the responsibility of the school to provide that opportunity should the placement be appropriate, regardless of English proficiency.

We must all be clear that lack of proficiency in English does NOT mean that students are "low" in ability or unable to learn higher-level concepts given appropriate supports. Not knowing English represents nothing at all except that one does not have proficiency in a language; there is absolutely no connection to intelligence or aptitude. ESL instruction is <u>not</u> supplemental or intervention; it is protocol and pedagogy that supports the acquisition of English and provides access to grade-level curricula. In order to provide equity for all students, one must give opportunities for learning to MLs that are comparable to their native-English-speaking peers.

What questions are acceptable for teachers to ask?

Some students are very forthcoming with their past experiences and others prefer to keep them in a reserve to themselves. I often start with a writing prompt in the primary language of the Newcomers soon after they have settled in, providing them with the opportunity to take ownership of the decision of sharing their story. Whether or not the teacher knows the language, it is crucial to encourage the student to use it to express themselves if that is what is comfortable for them. "Describe yourself." "Describe a time during which you experienced a big change." "Describe the best time in your life." "What do you like to do in your free time?" "What do you enjoy learning?" It's important to give students a voice, especially ones for whom it may have been silenced temporarily, but also give them the option to not exercise that right yet if they are not ready. By giving them that spot in the "driver's seat," students can write that narrative on their own terms.

There is thought now that teachers should not ask something like, "What do you want your teachers to know about you?" People feel that teachers are digging for unfortunate stories that students may (or may not!) have had. It is important to understand that teachers may not be equipped to deal with what the students have to share. However, I think it depends upon the student and the situation. I have done this in the past and have received very insightful academic comments from students. ***"I would tell her that I love social studies and I like to read stories about history."*** If this question is formed as an opportunity to share for a student who may not tend to volunteer to speak in front of the class, it can be very useful. ***"I like it when the teacher reads to us."*** This sort of opportunity to share one's thoughts or wishes can be powerful, but I now know that is best when kept to academics.

A student's legal or immigration status is **never** something that teachers should broach. If the student has concerns and would like to speak with a teacher about it, that would be absolutely reasonable, as long as the teacher understands that it is their responsibility to help make the child feel safe and accepted. Personal politics or feelings about immigration policies have no place when dealing with children in this way. Period.

Talking about family may also be a tricky subject for our Newcomers. Very often there are family members who were left behind before making the trip to the United States. ***"I felt so sad because I had to leave my little brother and I was not going to be able to see him again"***—translated. Other family dynamics may include the child being sent with a family member or as an Unaccompanied Minor to a parent or family member whom the child does not know because the family member had come to the country years before. There are times in which talking about family is a sensitive subject for our students and their families, for more reasons than we can imagine. Projects like family trees or interviews of family members should be treated with caution.

I typically do not address anything in terms of religion with my students, but before holidays or birthdays, I often reflect with students on the notion of choice in terms of participation. I discuss the usual ways in which the holidays are acknowledged within the school community and let the students know their options in terms of participation (or not). This could be wearing costumes at Halloween, celebrating birthdays, or singing songs for December holidays. ***"In my religion I cannot celebrate birthdays because that's the rule. But sometimes, in my old country my mom would spend the day with me and it is special. But now in America she works on my birthday and we***

don't do nothing." It's important not to take a student's preference for not participating in traditional activities personally and respect the choice of the student (or family) to decline.

When deciding whether one should ask a question or request information from Newcomers, one should reflect upon the purpose of the question. Is the answer going to inform instruction or allow us to help the child in school? Would the information be beneficial to the child if the teacher knows it? Are we giving the child the opportunity to choose the information to be shared? Or is the questioning simply satisfying the educator's personal curiosity? If the purpose reflects the needs of the student, then that is something for the educator to consider.

Not always shared experiences

Many teachers rely on the phrase *"I'm sure you've learned this before."* The problem is that it's very possible that students have not had the same types of experiences in education. This is certainly not to say that education in some places is "less than" other places, but there certainly may be focus on different material, skills, topics, or teaching styles. Spiraling curricula are helpful for reinforcing concepts that we tend to build upon in subsequent grades, but teachers cannot assume that students have previously learned this information.

Schools in the United States place much value on collaboration as an integral part of learning. This may be in direct contrast with many experiences in other countries, as are many other "norms" in our classrooms. To expect Newcomers to automatically understand how to navigate these different styles is not culturally responsive. As every country is different, I suggest teachers research some of the practices in the countries of your Newcomers so they are cognizant of how much support they may need in their classrooms. I have used this information as a great source of reflection, both on my own teaching style and my expectations for my diverse students.

While we look for the positives in those backpacks of experiences on which to build, sometimes students come to us with many challenges to overcome. Y came to the United States from another country as a 13-year-old and was placed in 6th grade. [This is not currently considered to be positive educational practice, as we should place students in the grade that is appropriate to their age, so they can interact with their peers and have access to grade-level curricula.] She was not literate in her first language and had not been to school since she was five, for a variety of reasons. Perhaps because of this, Y had very little interaction with other people in her lifetime, particularly children. She was scared and often cried, as each interaction was something she couldn't understand. After a few weeks, the school allowed Y to come in the afternoon and attend two small classes and then stay after school until 5 p.m. with her ESL teacher, Sarah. Y responded well to this type of schedule, in which her time in large groups was limited, and Sarah could really focus on language and life skills with her. Although these types of schooling situations may not be ideal for all students and we certainly do not want to isolate children, sometimes schools must think outside the box to meet individual needs of students.

Reflections discussion:

Reflection 1: We so rarely stop to think about our own traditions or culture that it may have been difficult for us to think of something strange in our own family. Often, we only notice when we realize that our tradition differs from someone else's. I really think nothing of most of the things we did growing up; they were just "normal" for me. Sitting around a tree that was cut down to put inside our house with presents that were magically placed there while I was sleeping? Or a large, somewhat creepy bunny sneaks into my house at night and hides candy and eggs for us? Both intruders are met with excitement and anticipation, not alarm. What's strange about that? And let's not get started about dressing up in costumes and begging strangers for candy—especially as we teach our children never to accept candy from strangers!

It's easier if I focus on traditions I intentionally made as an adult with my own family—most of which were in reaction to a different tradition. For instance, I am not a huge fan of fish, so I don't host Christmas Eve in the manner of some of my friends and family in the typical Italian way. Instead, we have all appetizers and desserts (junk food) on this day as we prepare for a beautiful meal at my sister's house and dessert and family time at my sister-in-laws' house the following day. What was my answer to not enjoying seafood is now the way my children celebrate Christmas Eve year after year.

Our students have cultures that are perfectly normal to them and that are woven through the thread of their family. I recall teaching high school and several of my students were fasting during the day during Ramadan. It was difficult on them, as it can be for anyone who cannot eat as per their usual routine. Rather than judging them or their families (as some teachers who don't understand the cultural importance of this ritual may do), these students need our support and respect. Similarly, I have heard the Day of the Dead festivities and traditions criticized by those who just don't understand the beauty of the experiences of those who celebrate.

One more point to clarify the acceptance of different traditions: There should be no judgment. I read recently that someone was critical of people who are not of Mexican or Central American descent who began their own way of celebrating Day of the Dead in their own families. This person felt that they are appropriating a culture that is not their own when they celebrate historically Hispanic holidays. However, it is perfectly acceptable for our MLs' families to celebrate Thanksgiving or other holidays that are new to them (or people almost resent it if they see that families do not celebrate these holidays in their "new" country). We must also be cognizant of how we represent these holidays in school (especially at the primary level) to ensure that no child is excluded if they do not celebrate. If any family chooses to share or mix cultural traditions—or maintain their own with fidelity—it is personal to them without judgment from anyone else.

Encouraging students to share their traditions and cultures and celebrating differences is a powerful way to connect with them and learn from one another. If we establish that environment that we can all learn from and respect one another's cultures and languages, we set the stage for powerful connections and pride in one's traditions across the board.

Reflection 2: This year my students completed an assignment of choosing five words that describe themselves, and it was so interesting to see the ways that they chose to represent themselves compared to how teachers described the same students. For example, one teacher described a student very differently from how he saw himself:

> Teacher: ESL student, Spanish-speaker, soccer player
>
> Carlos: Hondureño (from Honduras), buen hermano (good brother), Bad student (he said this in English), Quiero aprender inglés (I want to learn English), Quiero ser feliz (I want to be happy), fútbolista (soccer player)

After doing this activity, I was happy to see that the teacher knew that this student was on the soccer team for the school (knowing things that are important to him outside of class), but I really felt that giving the student the opportunity to identify for himself gave us insights into his feelings about himself and his role in life. I thought it was interesting that he called himself a "bad student" in English. Had he heard himself being described that way in English? Or was it that he wanted to be sure he was understood? Additionally, he focused on his goals (learning English and being happy). I have often seen very intelligent and motivated students who have difficulties with the way they are being taught in school. Some people are very capable of learning but struggle with test-taking and memorization. Add learning a second language to the mix, and this may be this student. Another thing to consider would be what would be the cause of this student feeling like a bad student; was he "bad" in his native country or does his lack of English proficiency affect his efficacy in learning?

I also loved how the student included things that he wants to achieve and his feelings about describing himself. Being happy and learning English must be things that are really important to him for him to include them in such a short list of descriptions of himself. Are these things that they talk about in his home? As I read the list, I wondered if he thinks these things would be dependent upon each other, but either way, I thought the inclusion of these was very telling.

Also interesting is how his teacher reflected on his eligibility as an "ESL student" while he talked about how he "wants to learn English." Do we see our students as their potential or their labels? It seems that Carlos is focused on his journey to bilingualism while his teacher thought of his placement.

How we feel different from the "norm" often shows up in some of the ways we identify ourselves. My race or ethnicity is not something that I immediately think of when describing myself; however, sometimes if a person of color were to answer the same prompt, being Latinx, Asian, or Black (or other races) might figure prominently in their identification of themselves. This identification of oneself is so powerful and allows us to articulate what are the things that best capture our essence.

We sometimes forget to give students the chance to reflect on feelings about themselves or ways to express things that are important to them, even if it's something that is not required to be handed into the teacher. Giving opportunities for perspectives about how children feel about themselves can help teachers understand them better and meet them where they feel that they are in terms of learning. An interesting activity may be to give this sort of reflection about themselves at different points of the year to see how their descriptions change over time, as well as the choice of language students use when writing about themselves.

For a checklist of considerations for these students, please see "Unpacking the Suitcase" in the appendix.

3

WHAT ARE THINGS TO DO IMMEDIATELY UPON ARRIVAL?

A Newcomer's arrival day may be compared to a visit to an amusement park funhouse. Nothing makes sense and things keep coming out at you in your face. A mixture of apprehension, terror, and excitement could explain the feelings of that first day.

Reflection questions:

- Is there a story behind your given name (or those of family members)? How does your name connect you to family or your ethnic background—or how does it not?
- Imagine a time in which you are on a road trip and are anxiously looking for a place to stop and eat. What are some possible conversations you could have with your trip companions and what would be the tone of those exchanges?

> ***"I never knew that I was coming to this country where I'm now. I had to say goodbye to all the people I love because my mom said, "Nos Vamos A Ir De Viaje" [We are going to take a trip] just me and her without my brother it was horrible because I knew it was the last time I was going to see my brother."***

In this chapter, you will find a working list of things to keep in mind in order to immediately help Newcomers acclimate to school and things to keep in mind during the first days. Based on the individual needs of each student, some activities may be necessary and others may not. A "Newcomer Packet" may be a way to share some of this type of information, especially if it's available in the native language of your student.

Welcome!

Many of us may never experience something akin to what our Newcomers and SLIFE do when they first enter our classrooms. There are many emotions that our students are sure to be feeling, and it is our responsibility to alleviate what we can for them. According to Salva and Matis (2017), *"The value of providing a warm, welcoming environment for new SLIFE arrivals to your classroom cannot be overemphasized"* (p.16). I am not being overly dramatic when I say that setting a positive tone for learning and education for these students may adjust the trajectory of their lives.

Maslow before Bloom?

It is absolutely crucial that education for Newcomers and SLIFE must be rigorous and include high-level skills and concepts. High expectations must be met with high standards for all students. We want to teach with dignity and ensure that our older learners are working with age-appropriate materials and grade-level curricula. With that being said, educators must consider all of the needs with which our Newcomers are contending and consider them while working with academics.

Many people have been using this phrase, "You gotta Maslow before you Bloom," to indicate that specific needs must be considered before students have the ability to work higher up on Bloom's Taxonomy. Maslow's Hierarchy of Needs (McLeod, 2020) has been construed in the past as a pyramid in which the basic needs of a person must be met before one can reach one's full potential. Physiological needs (water, food, warmth, rest) and safety needs are at the base of the pyramid and these needs were considered as needing to be fulfilled before other levels were met. "Full potential," in this case, would mean the ability to interact with others in creating and synthesizing, which are activities high on Bloom's Taxonomy.

While this is often used as defense that our students couldn't possibly handle higher level thinking or learning before their other needs are met—and it is absolutely reasonable to believe that hungry children are not able to learn optimally—it is now known that Maslow did not believe that these levels had to be met in a linear way (Kaufman, 2020). In other words, people do not just go through these levels once in their lives and then they reach the "pinnacle" of their existence; rather, they may flow from one level to another based on different experiences or events in their lives (Kaufman, 2020). As we may see with our Newcomers who are in a new phase in their lives, they may be moving in between several of those levels at any given time. Also critical to consider is the importance of connections and community to movement among these levels, also something for educators of Newcomers to keep in mind (Kaufman, 2020).

When Newcomers first arrive, teachers, counselors, nurses, and administrators must identify what critical needs these Newcomers have. Physiological needs must be addressed. This can include breakfast or lunch accessibility or assistance if they report they are homeless. Also, students who come to us under traumatic circumstances must feel safe and may be working within a level of Maslow's Hierarchy that is focused on that. Sometimes that feeling of safety does not come right away, but teachers can provide support and exposure to content and comprehensible input in the meantime. With this in mind, we can work with students in a variety of "levels" of needs without expecting them to achieve any given level before moving on to the next.

Sometimes, students' arrivals come with feelings of loss or sadness. "***One day when we were coming to America it was the saddest day of my life. We were leaving India, my village and where I had everything since I was born.***" Other students miss the family they left behind terribly and worry about their safety. The reason that some families leave their country may be because they were struggling or surviving horrible events. The preoccupations with these emotions may make it difficult for students to concentrate on learning new things.

With this being said, everything that our Newcomers do when they arrive is very complex and new for them, whether or not the activity ranks high on Bloom's questioning taxonomy. This is true for academic tasks as well as navigating this new life. The Newcomers are activating schema, creating new connections, making assumptions, and attempting to survive in a world with a new language. This is all extremely high-level thinking, even if the Newcomers are working mainly at the recall or comprehension phases academically—and exhausting!

Home Language Survey/Registration Information

While registering for school, parents fill out a Home Language Survey (or something akin to this). Sometimes this survey is completed at the school before any type of transcripts from prior schooling arrive. From this survey, teachers should be able to glean information to help begin assessing and deciding what services the student needs. Following are some crucial items to include on the survey:

- Language(s) spoken in the home by the student and by family members
- Country of origin
- Grades completed and amount of time elapsed since last attended school (if any)
- What type of school attended
- Any adults who understand or read English in the home/family (if applicable)
- Medical concerns (if any)
- Ways in which the school can contact the parents
- Parent commentary of student's experience with learning/schools
- Concerns or worries about school that parent would like to share

As the student registers for the first time in the school district, this is an opportunity to learn from their parents about things that may provide the background we need to determine how to help the student. It is here that we find out information about missing school or difficulties with academics in the student's home country. "***Learning has always been really difficult for her***"—translated. ***"My daughter was at the top of her class"***—translated. This type of information from parents does not really give us all we may learn from transcripts from previous schools, but it does give us the perspective of how the parent and child view their experiences with education.

When this information has been particularly useful are the times in which things just do not "make sense" in terms of what we may expect to see in progress or other indicators of understanding. Although as an ESL teacher and contact person, I look at the HLS right away for any "look-fors" that can assist me in helping the Newcomer, I do not typically share the information with the teaching staff unless I have some concerns or unanswered questions about a student. Times in which I share this information from the HLS may include when the student is doing so well that I may want to provide additional differentiation or because I have concerns that may be explained by what his parents said. Even though I use the HLS as a resource to give more background information about Newcomers, I am sure not to have any preconceived notions about the success of these students. No matter where our students begin or come from, their potential has no limits.

Learn your student's name. Really.

Learning someone's name is the most basic and personal way to show someone they are important. ***"I wish my teacher knows how to say my name right."*** Your students may have names that are unfamiliar to you. Learn them and practice them. I always attempt to pronounce my students' names, then ask them to pronounce them if I am unsure and write phonetically how they say them. Another suggestion may be to have the students record themselves saying their name (on FlipGrid?) so you have this as a reference. Correctly pronouncing a student's name may take several days for you to do naturally; this is absolutely necessary, and teachers doing this demonstrates the importance of the students in their class. This small practice is a way that you show your students that you value them and that you respect their language/background/culture/family.

Also, if possible, I ask for preferences with names, although students are so wanting to please that they sometimes say, "Whatever you like, teacher." So, I then ask what their parents call them, and get a better idea of the name the students may prefer. For example, some Hispanic families give their children the same first name, but they go by either their middle name or a combination of first and middle: Maria Teresa can be called Mayte or Teresa, while her sister, Maria Victoria can be Mavi or Victoria. In Chinese, their given name may be written last; teachers should clarify so they are not inadvertently calling children by their family name instead of their "given" name. I also had a Chinese student who was given a Mandarin name and an "English" name upon birth; we often practiced and wrote her Mandarin name, but she had a clear preference for her English name. Obviously I respected that.

Really learning students' names is really something about which to be really careful, as the name the teacher calls a student may become the student's name at school from that point on with all classmates. The feeling attached to the way people use and pronounce one's name is directly related to how willing one is to engage in and take risks within the situation. That feeling of acceptance and respect for students' names contributes to an environment in which students will take risks in learning.

Melissa found that she and her colleagues would occasionally see the same "Fnu" (Fuh-noo) in the electronic grade book at the beginning of the year. She, along with her fellow teachers, thought it was simply a name with which she was not familiar from a different language. When she would ask students about the pronunciation, they would never correct her...until she learned that it was not a name at all. It stands for First Name Unknown. Now, when Melissa sees this, she immediately asks for the student by the child's last name and writes down how the student would like to be addressed. One of her students later told her that it was an issue between the name on her passport and the name that was given on her birth certificate; certainly, her name is "known," but the paperwork just had to be verified.

The moral of this story is that even the most culturally sensitive teachers hit bumps in the road sometimes. As Melissa did, adjust your practice and keep the child's dignity the priority. In other words, learn your student's correct or preferred name and use it frequently —and with a smile!

Be sure the students have a visual with their name and classroom number/teacher on it with them at all times.

If possible, teachers should allow students to write this information themselves and practice asking for and responding with this information in English. They will encounter people who don't know who they are during their first days and this can help them answer questions about who they are and where they belong should they get flustered. Picture this student (see below) being asked questions by an administrator or faculty member; the visual will provide crucial information if needed.

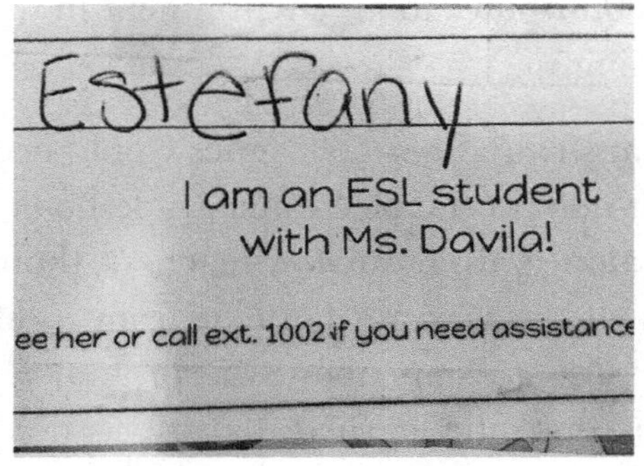

Little things like this can help alleviate some stress and anxiety for students within those first days. Some may view this technique as a crutch and would like for students to be forced to use English right away; I disagree and believe this process will guide Newcomers with getting comfortable quickly and taking risks more readily. If God forbid, there is an emergency in the students' first days in school, this will assist in identifying them and helping them get to their teacher.

Ashley also provides Newcomers with a ring of common phrases with visuals for them to take with them from class to class. In the first days, the students will just point to show their teacher what they are trying to communicate, but very quickly they get the confidence to practice the phrases before asking their teachers in the target language. This type of scaffold empowers the students to produce in the target language without fear of being misunderstood.

Ensure that every student understands procedures for leaving the room (bathroom, nurse, drink) and that it's okay to ask.

If it's possible, teachers can actually walk students to the nurse for an introduction, so they understand what the office looks like, even if they don't remember how to get there. This kind of process provides opportunities for students to bond with others (e.g., nurse, secretary, principal) and to introduce them to people who can later greet them or help them when necessary. Classmates can accompany the Newcomers on future visits, but at least the Newcomers will have prior knowledge of what the places look like. If later there is an issue in which they have to go to the nurse (office or guidance), it will be a familiar place and hopefully they can go with less anxiety of the unknown.

If you have certain times or procedures for leaving the room, please ensure that your Newcomers know what to do to use the facilities or leave the room if necessary. Patience is key here because they are learning so much at once that they may not initially understand the procedures or what to do in the event of an emergency. Newcomers may enter the class during the school year (when the rest of the class has a handle on procedures), so teachers must be aware that there will be a learning curve for the Newcomers. Again, dignity and feelings of security are first priority; classroom management/procedures will come.

If there are lockers that are available for use for the students, they may have to be accompanied to the locker for the first several times. While many students who are not new to the district (but new to lockers) may struggle at first, Newcomers need to understand that they have assistance with these types of procedures if needed and that they are able to keep their things safe from being stolen, yet accessible to them. When one moves to a new country and may not have been able to take many of their possessions, this feeling that their items are safe can feel very important.

Go over snack and lunch procedures and provide support as needed.

Every school has procedures for snacks and lunch, and these may be the first opportunities Newcomers have to rest and possibly interact with peers. Although this seems like it isn't that important, these times can make or break the child's first days. If snacks are eaten in class, make sure the student knows what's acceptable to bring.

If it's a possibility that the Newcomer may qualify for free or reduced lunch, please help obtain the paperwork to send home. I also always try to go to the cafeteria myself to ensure the Newcomer is able to access the food and find some friendly students in the cafeteria for any needed assistance. Information about available food in the school may require a phone call home to explain, but it is so important to ensure that students have access to breakfast and lunch if necessary.

Finding a friendly—and perhaps a bilingual—student with whom a Newcomer can sit at lunch may provide a connection for support throughout the day. A smile and some assistance at this part of the day is so valuable. Please communicate with teachers and staff on lunch duty to keep a Newcomer's teacher informed if there are any concerns in the lunchroom. Donna and Nancy both saw that some of our new students were eating alone during different lunch periods. They enlisted bilingual buddies to help communicate with the students but later spoke with the ESL teachers to help. One of our students preferred the quiet of eating alone and reading, which we totally understood and appreciated; the quiet downtime helped her calm the chaos of the rest of her day. Another student gratefully accepted the invitation to sit with other students, which was facilitated by the ESL teachers. Sometimes students only need help in noticing that someone is being left behind or alone; once someone helps them with that, they let kindness lead the way.

Student Voice

Voice is power. Power to express oneself, power to control what people know about oneself, power to have a record of one's feelings and experiences. Our students have lived through experiences that are unique to them and have stories to be told. As others read their words, their powerful words, their bit of history is being shared. That is the purpose of this book: to empower teachers to empower their students. They are empowered by what they choose to share and what they decide to write (and what *not* to write!). We can learn much from them by just giving them the opportunity to use their Voice.

A first step may be to provide the students with an opportunity to write something about themselves in their primary language or with any English they know. A Newcomers' writing can provide you with much insight into their experiences or information about them. Writing about ourselves is ensuring that the topic is familiar to the writers and this can give them the opportunity to reflect about themselves. The most important thing is that the students will determine what it is that they choose to share about themselves. They are in control. Use Google translate if necessary to read it; however, refrain from corrections. (Louder for the people in the back: Refrain from corrections!) We do not know the educational background of the Newcomers, and we want to be sure that we are creating positive and empowering experiences with literacy. The message, at this time, is so much more important than the mechanics.

Some of our Newcomers may come to us without the knowledge of writing, even in their native language. Obviously, this does not exclude them from having something important to share. If drawing is an appropriate means of expression, that absolutely can be encouraged. We then give them the opportunity to record their voice in whatever language is dominant to them (or a mixture of languages if that is what they prefer). Using technology or native speakers of the language is key to understanding what is being shared, but the experience of expressing the information (using their Voice) is actually more important than deciphering what was said. Many teachers may prefer to record the actual voices of all Newcomers because the actual sound of their voice talking about themselves or their experiences is powerful.

For those students for whom writing is a challenge in any language, creating documents with images or drawings is also a way to help them express themselves. Rachel created a digital vision board with her students that did not include any words, just images. She was then able to explain her use of each image verbally and with scaffolded use of English as necessary. She also focused the images on her vision board to show her learning and reading to model that we all can include them in our goals.

We also want to take any opportunity to give the students Voice and chances to reflect about themselves and choice about what they would like to share with their new teachers or classmates. They are starting fresh and are able to control the information that people have about them. What they have to share is valuable and interesting. What a powerful thing it is to have such control over what you share with people.

If the Newcomers write, their writing sample can also be viewed as a benchmark writing sample to recall the level of writing when they arrived. It is also crucial to note that this writing sample should be viewed from a growth mindset—this is what they can do *now* and we will improve from there. Also, most critically, what these children have to say—the content—is far more important than the mechanics through which they express it. Again, their Voice is key.

Translanguaging (switching between languages) is a valid phase in language acquisition.

Es cuando estoy leyendo (It's when I'm reading) the book and soñando (dreaming) of other places.

Translanguaging is the process of intentionally using words from both the primary and the target language in order to express oneself. In the past, this was referred to as "code switching" and was rather controversial. Some people claimed that it is a shortcut in language learning that is detrimental to progress and that relying too much on one's dominant language would impede acquisition or learning the target language. Others maintained that it helps language learners express themselves in ideas and concepts that may be beyond their language proficiency. It builds confidence in both expressing in the target language and understanding of content. Today, experts tend to agree with the latter, stating that this phase in language acquisition allows learners to produce language and communicate in whichever language comes naturally to them while acquiring additional languages.

Please allow students to leverage their native language in order to acquire English and learn content. Native language literacy skills assessments are helpful if available. Don't assume our Newcomers have on-level literacy skills (especially SLIFE), but whatever skills they already have can be used to develop skills in English. It is absolutely crucial to ensure students know that we understand that they have valuable skills in their native language, whether or not they are confident in their level of literacy. **We do not assume that, because they do not have proficiency in English yet, they are not intelligent or capable of learning.** Their native language is a treasure that they will have for their entire lives and must be valued as such.

As our students are gaining vocabulary in English, we can reasonably expect them to utilize those words in English as they are communicating in both languages. In content areas, the words on the multilingual word wall or keywords in the unit can be assessed for accuracy, as well. However, if students change back and forth between languages, this might be just where they are in language acquisition. We may also find that older students are able to write more in English in terms of using vocabulary than speak; they have more time to process while writing and may be able to "find" the words in their language repertoire more easily when writing. With that being said, grammar when writing may come last, but it will come eventually with a healthy mixture of explicit instruction and comprehensible input (see Chapter 7).

As we keep discussing growth mindset, this is the point at which we understand that there is more knowledge that learners have than what can be demonstrated by their command of English. They know many, many things and should not be relegated to communicating only what their target language proficiency allows. Translanguaging empowers learners as they take risks in producing words in the target language, even if these words are surrounded by words in their primary language. As they progress and add more words in the target language, confidence grows with vocabulary. Teachers who accept answers using translanguaging are supporting their students in both content understanding and language acquisition.

One final thought about Translanguaging: When any speakers use translanguaging, this often does not indicate that they are a language learner or that they do not have proficiency in one language or another. It is not always part of a transition or acquisition of language. Rather, for many people, translanguaging is a way of expressing themselves, using the parts of whatever language that fit their purpose at that moment. Translanguaging is a powerful, intentional way to use language that transcends cultures and languages. When our students (MLs or not) partake in this, they are participating in a process and a community of language speakers. Again, people are using their Voice to express themselves in an authentic way. Amazing stuff, in my opinion.

Emergencies

Fire drills, lockdowns, evacuations, and other emergency drills may cause anxiety in Newcomers for many reasons. They may trigger memories of past traumas that they have experienced in life prior to arrival at your school. ***"I still remember this day when there was an earthquake and I was in school and I was crying because I was worried about my brothers. When we heard the fire drill sound I wanted to run to see my brothers but my teacher told me not to go."*** We also have been seeing an influx of students who are leaving their homes following natural disasters, such as hurricanes and earthquakes, which obviously can have some lasting emotional or physical effects. They may not understand that what they are now experiencing is only a drill and not a real emergency. Students who have anxiety about their legality and safety in this country may be scared that these drills are connected to the police raids that they fear so much. We have had drills in which people are banging on the doors of the classroom to see if the teacher will open the door, without thinking about the trauma they may be inflicting on the children inside. These drills may also just be a frightening experience (the noise, the rush to get out of the building, having to hide in the classroom).

Reviewing and explaining emergency procedures before any drill is important for Newcomers to alleviate concerns. Some schools include information of this type in a "Newcomer Handbook," which they share with the student and parent at registration before they arrive on the first day. This handbook should be translated into the languages of the community. Other schools provide video explanations on district websites of what happens during specific kinds of drills. If teachers discuss the different kinds of drills beforehand, including using visuals, Newcomers will not be taken by surprise when they do experience them.

Needless to say, if there truly is an emergency, teachers must be sure to calmly support all children, but especially Newcomers. By announcing the type of emergency (e.g., evacuation, lockdown) and the destination at the first signal of the event, the teacher will help to calm the Newcomers' nerves. ***"Oh, I understand what we are doing. We did this for hurricanes all the time in my country"***—translated. Assigning a peer buddy during emergency drills is also a way to ensure Newcomers understand where to go and what to do, and aren't frightened. Whatever is effective for the safety and feelings of security for these students is important to address immediately upon entry into school.

Snow days, emergency closings, and how to get the information must be explained if applicable. Schools cannot assume that families listen to the radio stations, have access to the district website, or that they understand robocalls that broadcast in English. There must be an expressed plan for early dismissals, as well, as many parents work second shifts or while their children are in school. If there are ways to get this information other than through the internet, that should be addressed.

Technology access

Modern technology can now provide for us a bridge of communication even if we do not share the same language at that time. Upon entering the school, teachers should obtain passwords/computer access as soon as possible and show students Google translate or other useful sites to help empower students with a means of communication. Teachers can also use technology as a way to provide images, videos, maps and other types of visuals to help students make connections between the concepts being taught and the target language. Melissa uses Google Meets as a way to connect with her Newcomers who are in different classes. Students are able to get the attention of the teacher, put closed captions on to see what she is saying (and are able to translate it) and can "chat" in a low-risk environment. She also has a specific Google Classroom for this group, with assignments that have the students working on the same objectives as the other students, but with more scaffolds and language supports.

With that being said, Newcomers may or may not come to us having any computer skills. This can provide many challenges, as many assessments and collection of data take place using technology. It's important to keep this in mind as educators understand that variables other than academics may interfere with these assessments if students aren't adept with computers. If handheld translators are available, teaching students how to use them would be very useful in situations both inside and outside the classroom.

Working on technology skills with Newcomers is a worthwhile investment, as it can help them build schema in the content area, as well as assist them in understanding and communicating in the target language. While teaching in the virtual-learning model, we had a number of students who entered our classes as Newcomers to our country. Using a visual of the computer and keyboard, we were able to help these students virtually learn how to use the computer keys and Google Classroom. In my experience, these students are so motivated to learn the technology that they pick it up very quickly.

District-specific questions

Uniforms or dress codes are something about which all new students must be explicitly directed. Many Newcomers will have had these in their previous schools, but they need to know the specifics of their new school. If there are options to reduced-price uniforms available, that information should be shared with parents at registration. Information about uniforms or dress codes must be at least provided before the student begins; no children want to feel that they "stick out" in an uncomfortable way on their first day of school. Patience must be used if Newcomers make mistakes with the uniforms at first, again using visuals to communicate the required clothing.

Calendar information, including half days and holidays, must be given to the parents or guardians upon registration with someone explaining how to access the information in their native language. Don't assume that a student knows when there are scheduled days off from school or when there is an early dismissal.

Following a schedule is a challenge for all students as they move into the upper grades, let alone students who are new to this type of school environment. Enlisting "peer buddies" to accompany them from one class to the next is crucial to keep our Newcomers from feeling anxious or lost. Some districts assign these buddies by the student's schedule and others have school leaders whose job it is to help students who are new to the school. Either way, fostering connections with different students is beneficial for our Newcomers.

Beginning/end times and arrival/dismissal procedures need to be explained, especially if the student's family has children in different schools within the district. The importance of being on time for school may also have to be addressed, as rules and norms for punctuality differ in different countries (or districts!). If there are opportunities for after-school help or tutoring, being specific with the parents of Newcomers about the importance and logistics are crucial.

Attendance policies may be different from our Newcomers' previous country in terms of the number of acceptable absences and reasons to miss school. Some district nurses put together a visual to help parents understand when students should not attend school for a variety of reasons. While consistent attendance is important, we must be certain to communicate that children must stay home if they are sick for the safety of everyone. Vaccinations are also important for parents to understand and often students cannot begin school until their records are up to date.

Reflection discussion:

Reflection 1: A person's name is the most individual thing one can learn about a person. Acknowledging students by name and with a smile provides them with a sense of belonging in the school community. But names are even more than that. In some families, names that are given to children are very important to their family, religion, or culture. Some name their children after grandparents, saints' names, or names that are culturally significant. ***"My name is a mixture of both of my parents' names." "I am named after my sister who passed away." "My sister is named after the patron saint of El Salvador."*** —all translated. To simplify someone's name (*Can I just call you Joe?*) to make it "easier" to pronounce is stealing a piece of their identity away.

Asking students about their name (first or last) and any stories or information they know about their names can help you get insight into their family or culture. ***"My parents named me after a character on their favorite TV show"***—translated. You may get really fun or different stories that have to do with students' names that help you connect or forge relationships better.

Learning their names and proper pronunciation (*Keep correcting me until I get it right!*) shows that they are welcomed in the school community as themselves—and not a pretend person who "fits in" with any preconceived notion of who they should be in their new school. According to Winokur (2020), that feeling of belonging must be met before one can begin to progress with learning. When we intentionally work to pronounce students' names correctly and include them in the school community, they know that they are accepted for who they are and from where they come...and where they are going.

Reflection 2: "Are we there yet?" If you have ever taken a road trip with a child, I'm sure you have heard that. The tone of the question may be fraught with anxiety (read: whining) while the answer from the adults may be short on patience with their repeated replies.

Although these trips may seem much longer from the perspective of a child than it may seem to an adult, I do think this repeated question is more looking for reassurance of what is coming next than actually for a number of minutes left in the trip. The adults are able to see the mile markers or know what time the next stop will be; the children are along for the ride with little information other than what the adults share. When students are new to the routine of school in a different country, they may feel this same insecurity about what is coming next—but without the language to keep asking for that reassurance.

Having visuals of the daily schedule and bilingual buddies to help our Newcomers through the first days and weeks helps alleviate some of the tension and anxiety that they may feel with the unknown. These first days in the new country may seem interminable, and understanding more about the schedule may help the Newcomer get through the day. Some of these students may also be food insecure, which brings another dimension to the anxiety of when the next time they will eat will be. Students may also be unable to tell time on an analog clock, which can add to the uncertainty of what will happen next.

Remembering the way it feels when one does not have certainty about how one's day is going to play out is important for teachers as they seek to connect with how these students are feeling.

The schooling systems and norms in a new country may be very different from what our Newcomers have experienced. When we keep in mind the perspective of children who are feeling anxious and uncertain, we intentionally look for ways to show them they are safe and welcomed with open arms.

For an example of questions to include in a Home Language Survey and a reference guide for introductory activities, please see the appendix.

4

ACKNOWLEDGING, CELEBRATING, AND APPRECIATING CULTURE

"Why would I have interest in this book? These characters are nothing like me. I don't care about what happens in the story."

— *Ryan, age 14*

Reflection Questions:

- How are the books covered in grade-level curricula chosen? How often are the curricula updated? Who chooses these books and are there rationales?
- How are classroom library books chosen and organized?

Representative & Connective Pedagogy (derived from Culturally Responsive Pedagogy)

It is important that schools and teachers create an environment in which all students (and staff!) feel as if they belong there. This can be achieved through reflection upon the climate of the school. Representative & Connective Schools:

- empower all students and fosters connections among them;
- acknowledge, value, and celebrate the diversity of students;
- bridge gaps between languages, cultures, perspectives;
- create a culture of acceptance and belonging in the classroom/school;
- provide an environment in which all students feel comfortable taking risks;
- encourage collaboration with diverse learners;
- include literature that represents all students in curricula;
- analyze curricula and ensure that different perspectives are represented;
- build schema for all students in diverse topics/cultures;
- provide access for families within the school culture;
- ensure that all students have extracurricular opportunities

Mirrors versus Windows? Sliding doors? Prisms?

We have often spoken about the concept of literature (and classroom activities!) needing to be more of a mirror than a window. This analogy was first introduced by Emily Style (1988) in the National SEED Project. A student "sees" oneself in the literature that is like a mirror and is more of an outsider looking in (through the window) if the literature does not reflect the student's own culture. We've seen the visual of the very sad child looking through the window but not included. This is an excellent illustration of the feelings that one may have if one does not share culture or traits with the characters or settings in the books in the classroom or school library.

Although I don't think it was Style's intention, many people tend to interpret this as a disservice to our MLs if all of the books do not represent them or their culture. I absolutely agree that positively representing all cultures is crucial for the well being of all students. Through the representation of their culture in literature (and within the school community), students can see themselves in other situations and other places and this can plant the seeds for where they see themselves in the world and in their future. This can also help foster a sense of belonging within the group and pride in one's own culture.

> ***"I've never been able to see about my own experience like this book. I never read something that tells the story of immigrants so real before. People just don't understand what they go through. It's good to have people read about it. I felt this in my stomach as I read it."***

This student was so excited to be able to relate to a story of a family immigrating into the United States and immediately began talking about it and comparing it to her own experiences. There was a passion for reading that book that she didn't show with other books. This book may prove to be a challenging read for this student, but she clearly has the motivation and excitement to continue reading even if she has difficulties.

An important point about having multicultural literature in the classroom library (and school libraries!) is that, although it is crucial to include books from many different cultures, it's essential to ensure that the libraries represent the *current student population*. While it is interesting and absolutely appropriate to have books about specific South American native tribes or even African folktales, one shouldn't ignore Asian books if they represent part of the school population. In fact, the books should mirror the population: If the district is 70 percent Hispanic, then there should be a similarly large number of books in the libraries representing those many cultures from Spanish-speaking countries. And if the cultural dynamic changes often in a school or district, then books should be added annually! Also critical to note: Authentic multilingual books are necessary in these libraries as well. A library cannot have too many diverse books nor too many options for students to read! However, the books that are added should authentically provide representation for the students, not be a whim of someone's interest.

With that being said, providing literature that is *always* a "mirror" isn't ideal nor necessarily possible. For one thing, most likely any given class can have several cultures represented, especially classes with MLs. Whenever literature is a "mirror" for one culture, it may be a "window" for the others. We cannot even always assume that children who come from the same country have the same perspectives or experiences. Although we strive to provide literature with which students can make connections, this is not always possible. Sometimes, these "window" stories give perspective to students about one another's cultures, which is a very positive way to foster understanding and relationships within the school or classroom community. And this would be where the "sliding doors" come in: a way to enter into another's culture through literature and really gain an understanding of one another and of different countries and cultures around the world. "Sliding doors" allow access to stories that differ from our own, but they are written in a way that includes the reader in the experience and gives insight into lives that may be different from the reader's. These "doors" invite us in and broaden our perspectives on life.

Krisnaswami (2019) adds another perspective through which we may view literature: a prism. "A prism can slow and bend the light that passes through it, splitting that light into its component colors." Likewise, when reading a book that can encourage us to question what we have always known, rethink our assumptions of the world, and maybe change us for the better after reading it, that would be a prism. When I think back to books that have affected me so powerfully, I really do think there is such value in books that may open our eyes to things we never knew or understood before.

When we think of diverse literature, we most often think of ethnicity, culture, or language. However, diverse literature also is inclusive of differing abilities, family structures, gender roles, LGBTQIA+ characters, religions, social class, language, and many other differences. When students find literature that reflects their lives or experiences—or gives insight into others' experiences in an inclusive way—they are able to really engage in literacy that lights a fire inside them. It is within these experiences (these "fires") that children build their stamina and skills in literacy.

Sometimes, however, the cultures of our students are represented in a stereotypical or negative way in literature, and this is something about which educators must be very careful. Although it is not necessary to ensure that all stories read in the classroom are multicultural, it is beneficial if the books chosen do not perpetuate misconceptions about the cultures of the students in the community, even if they are considered to be "classics" by many. I'm not suggesting that all books should be censored or thrown out of classroom libraries, but as teachers choose stories for read alouds (for example), it is often viewed as "endorsements" of those books. If there are questionable representations of groups of people in those books, students may feel that teachers are accepting and presenting those views as well.

Infusion of Culture in Content Classes

Making connections between languages and cultures in content-area classes is a key way to engage learners. For instance, while teaching about ancient civilizations in social studies, Allyssa connects the history of the Maya, Inca, and Aztec to those students whose families may come from the same area of the world. ***"I want Americans to know that Mexico has Aztecs, Maya and that they were very smart. That without them we have no calendar and no zero."*** Ashley has a multilingual word wall in science and anchor charts in the languages of her students. Students can refer to the same resources as their native-English-speaking peers, as well as identifying similarities in content-area cognates. Cognates are words that have similarities among languages—and they give opportunities for MLs to leverage their knowledge in their dominant language(s) to support their content-area understanding (*computadora/computer*). It's important to acknowledge that English does not share cognates with all languages, but there are instances in which similarities in words can be used to support some learners.

"***Learning about other countries and languages makes us a better country or world.***"

While creating word problems in math or sentences for spelling words, Kara and Gill use names from the classes and make sure that all students get represented. Looking to see who will be involved that day engages the students—especially when the problems are silly—and it "normalizes" names of different cultures. Students feel included as part of the classroom culture when their names are parts of the lesson.

One of my students made a connection with what the science teacher was teaching in class. ***"The teacher says that the sun isn't a living thing, but that is not what I learned in my country. The sun is a man and the moon is a woman. Sometimes they get along and sometimes they fight. When they fight, it's an eclipse. So,*** [laughing] ***I learned differently from a legend in my country"***—*translated.* This student couldn't wait to come up to me and tell me her background knowledge with this concept with a huge smile on her face. We laughed together and later I asked her to draw a representation of the legend for me to share with the teacher. I just was so delighted that she shared that connection from her home country with me and that we had the opportunity to spotlight it.

Art, music, and physical education teachers can also highlight content from the cultures of their students. Units on Lunar/Chinese New Year, Latin American music and painters, and Caribbean dance and sports provide students with perspectives outside their own. In art class, especially, students can create art that is meaningful to them personally or that represents their families or cultures--or that helps them learn about the diverse cultures of the world.

Keeping the experiences authentic and ensuring that different cultures are included throughout the year (and not just during certain months!) is key to creating a culturally inclusive environment. Allowing students to be "experts" and share their backgrounds in different areas is also a great way to give voice to students who may otherwise not feel confident enough to speak up.

Outside the Academics

There are several simple ways that school communities can celebrate the many different cultures that are represented by the students who attend. This is important to boost the positive feelings about diversity among the students and staff, rather than the feeling that one is an outsider on the edge of the community.

Bulletin boards and signs inside or outside the school are visible and noticeable ways that cultures and languages can be celebrated, and not only during the months that specifically celebrate those cultures. This can include scientists, artists, writers, or other people whose backgrounds represent those of the people in the school. Heather and Jacki engage students in creating things such as "Affirmation Stations," in which students leave notes in different languages that are positive messages that other students can take as encouragement as needed. Also, this year in my school, the staff and students all created posters of positivity, which represented different languages or quotes from different cultures to line the hallways with messages.

Even boards with "Welcome!" in various languages set the tone when someone enters the building that diversity is encouraged.

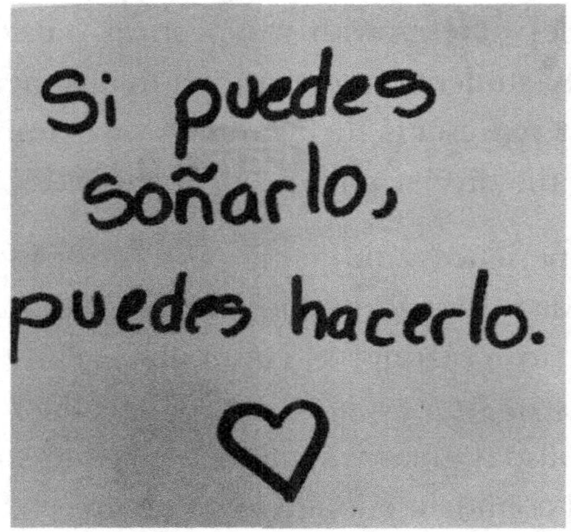

Inclusive assemblies are important to ensure that everyone benefits from the messages and entertainment. School-based chorus or band concerts can include songs from different countries or in different languages to expose all students to multicultural music or dance.

Something as simple as learning how to greet students in their primary language—or saying "Bless you" when they sneeze in their language—shows that you value them and their culture. Making that effort to include other cultures in these types of ways broadens the horizons of all of the students in the class. If the teacher does this, the other students will recognize the value and follow suit.

In some districts, parents are permitted to come into the classrooms and read to the students, even if it is in another language (virtual visits are wonderful, too!). Not only does this celebrate the traditional literacy of another culture, but it also provides the opportunity for students to feel pride and ownership of their language. Multicultural nights are also a great way to get family involved in celebrating the cultures of the community. Students, staff, and family members create tri-fold presentations, show artifacts, wear traditional dress, and maybe even cook foods that represent their families and cultures. People smile at one another and ask questions about each other's cultures; pride is bursting from all sides.

Morning announcements can also include other cultures, such as saying the date or greetings in other languages or sharing fun facts about countries that are represented within the school community. Students can be engaged in researching and sharing these bits of information. Multicultural music can also play in the hallways during dismissal or arrival, which can introduce students to different types of music, as well as helping maintain a positive climate in the school.

Let's face it: The more we learn about other cultures, the more we connect with one another. No longer do we speak in terms of "them" or "those people"; rather our pronouns switch to "we." It's this feeling of belonging that helps students engage in learning and becoming members of our school community (Winokur, 2020).

The policy of the school?

If there is no district-wide or school-wide policy about educating MLs, teachers are left to their own devices as to what type of support or instruction that they will use to meet their needs. There will be no consistency among classrooms, and people will feel as if it is an "option" whether or not they alter their normally scheduled "programming" to include MLs in their instruction. According to Cummins (2000), the protocol for educating MLs must be created for all classrooms, not just the ones in which teachers are inclined to adjust their teaching to meet their needs. These standards must be across the board and in every classroom in the school.

The responsibility for educating MLs must be at the district or school level, not only at the classroom level. It is at this level that curricula are considered, as well as staffing and professional development. With that being said, teachers are responsible for the implementation of this protocol in their individual classrooms without excuses. There is no one in the district who does not take responsibility for the education of these students.

There must be collaboration on the part of the teachers, administrators, staff, AND the students when working with MLs! That collaboration may look like any or all of the following:

- Teacher/Teacher
- Teacher/Educational Service Professional (ESP/Paraprofessional)
- Teacher/Student
- Student/ESP
- Student/Student
- Teacher/Administrator

Once everyone is knowledgeable about their role in the education of ALL students, all become stakeholders in inclusion for everyone in all activities in the classroom.

Keywords to remember

When reflecting upon how best to welcome and include culturally diverse students in our classroom, we can post a visual of the following words to keep our minds in focus:

accessibility: Ensuring that our school culture and curricula are accessible to all students, even those with diverse needs, provides a climate in which success is possible for everyone. Accessibility looks different for different students, but all objectives and learning targets should reflect accessibility for all students.

celebration: Every day should be a celebration of life, a celebration of diversity, a celebration that our students are there. Everyone is an "insider" when all cultures and successes are celebrated.

inclusivity: People won't beg to be included; often, they will sit on the sidelines and feel that they do not matter. This applies to classroom dynamics and to life in general. Just because students are present in a classroom does not mean that they are included. Teachers and administrators must ensure that MLs have access to the activities and curricula of grade-level classes.

representation: Reflections about our feelings about the diverse languages and cultures in our school community and if the stakeholders see the inherent value in such diversity are crucial conversations here. Educators must ensure that diversity is represented throughout the school and is a priority of the administration.

authenticity: Are literature choices authentically multicultural or are they included to check off a box? Do we only discuss African-American contributions in history, literature, or science in February? Hispanic Heritage is only included in September? I always connect this to Hollywood—are the actors who play Asian parts actually Asian or or are they Caucasian with makeup on? In schools, do we "do multiculturalism" just to say it's done? Or is it an integral part of the fabric of the school?

perspective: Are we genuinely interested in providing Voice for students to share their perspectives? Do we provide them the opportunity to read literature that represents them? Do we recognize that Hispanic cultures are very different from one another? Do we recognize that Asian, African, European, or Caribbean cultures are very diverse as well? Do our schools actually represent all of our students? And do all of our students understand the perspectives of one another?

value: Do we value ALL student Voice and agency? Is value quantified for different groups? Do we value the cultures of the minority or does our school follow the "majority rules" motto? What are some possible outcomes that are based on student perception of "value?"

advocacy: All young people need someone to advocate for them. Some people have their parents or their own cultural community that "go to bat" for them. Others need unlikely sources to advocate for them in ways that they may never have dreamt. Be that source. Be that teacher. It is your mission to fight for your students!

equity: Equity is manifested in a variety of ways in schools. Are grade-level curricula accessible to all students? Do students feel marginalized or engaged by their teachers and administrators? Are ESL (or special ed) classes in classrooms that have the materials and environment necessary for success? Are MLs considered to be a vital part of the school community? If diverse learners are included in general education classes, are they truly part of the class or simply sitting there? Do we have high expectations for all students?

dignity: Are challenges that some students face because of their cultures or socioeconomic status addressed with the dignity of the people involved in mind? If students are eligible for food programs to help their families or are in need of clothing or donations, are their needs met without public knowledge with respect to their dignity? Are our SLIFE and their possible learning challenges or differences viewed through a lens of dignity?

stereotype: If stereotypes permeate the community, the school may have an uphill battle changing those attitudes within the building...but it must be done. Students learn these attitudes quickly and internalize them, whether they are learning about their own culture or another. Change comes from the top. Be sure that the literature chosen in school does not perpetuate stereotypes of any kind.

racism: Children listen very carefully to what is being said by the adults in their lives. Informal dinner table talk is what shapes the perspective of children and this can be very powerful. After the election of 2016, some students ran through the halls of our middle school yelling disparaging comments about people of other ethnicities. In a very diverse school, this contributed to a culture of discord in the school. Other students were frightened about the future of themselves or their family, and the fact that this was how their peers felt about people "like them" was disheartening.

belonging: A feeling of belonging is not always as tangible as one would hope, especially for Newcomers or students who have moved from place to place. But that feeling can make the difference for so many things for our students. According to Winokur (2020), "People don't usually move out of their comfort zones unless they feel welcome, included, and accepted (p.80)". Those moves in which students are taking risks take them to where they can learn and grow. So, those activities in the classroom that are meant to help build connections and foster relationships are absolutely crucial to academic progress for all students.

compassion: This is where the supportive community comes in for our Newcomers and MLs. As teachers, we did a book club about *My Family Divided* by Diane Guerrero. Reading a story that may represent the experiences of some of our students' families really gave us a chance to share compassion for those in that situation. Some teachers had no idea about what experiences may reflect some of our students and their families. We may not know what these students carry in their backpacks, but we offer to help shoulder the load for them if we understand them better. And it makes all the difference.

Reflection discussion:

Reflection 1: Many students take the lead of their teachers when it comes to which books they read. Some feel that the teachers know best about which books are "good"; after all, they're the expert! (How many teachers read Harry Potter to their class only to have the students follow up independently with the rest of the series?? And how satisfying is that??) With this in mind, some districts update their language arts curricula regularly to ensure that students have exposure to current literature and a variety of genres.

However, some districts don't necessarily view the books covered in language arts as something that needs to change with the times (or population of students). Some teachers/curriculum writers feel that the "classics" which they have taught for years are great choices for now and for the years to come. After all, they know those stories inside and out and have plenty of activities to use while teaching them.

There are several aspects of books that I feel are important to consider when choosing a book to read as a class, especially one with MLs.

- Is this quality literature? Think of themes being important to the students, if the writing is rich and detailed, and the characters are solid. Is this book worth your (and their) time?
- Would this book be a window, mirror, or sliding door to my students? All are acceptable, surely, but keeping track of which types over the year are read in class is crucial. Diversity in this aspect of book choice cannot be ignored.
- I cannot emphasize this enough: Are there stereotypes of cultures in this literature? If there are mentions that are not essential to the story, am I able to make it a teachable moment? Does the representation of a particular group in a negative light outweigh the benefits of sharing this book with the class?
- Is the book's vocabulary meaningful for use today? Or is it full of outdated jargon that would not benefit the students to learn? (Think: jalopy)
- Would this book help build the schema of my students in different areas? Books that help give information that may be useful in different aspects of students' lives will give them more "bang for their buck."
- Rather than reading an entire book all the time, an option is

to read excerpts that help support the mini-lessons being taught. I do think it's important that students experience some books from beginning to end, but reading parts that are especially rich may expose them to more types of literature and provide authentic material for lessons. A healthy mix is a good option.
- Poetry and other types of literature can be used to expose students to different types of voice while also using shorter pieces to engage them. The concept of rhythm and rhyme in language is also very supportive of literacy and language acquisition.

While I completely agree that it is very important to expose students to classic books, I think that they can be one part of a diverse collection of literature that is covered in class. The importance of experiencing literature with diverse characters and written by diverse authors cannot be underestimated. And to have the teacher even read books about different cultures aloud to the class? What could possibly give more credence to the importance of those voices?

One final thought about choosing books: While some pieces of literature may not be the best choice for group read-alouds or assignments, there may certainly be a place in the classroom library for them. I am certainly not suggesting that we censor all books that do not "fit" into the categories above; rather provide them as an option for independent reading at the choice of the student.

Reflection 2: In terms of books in the classroom library, there are many schools of thought about how to organize them. Some teachers organize fictional books by reading level to allow students to find "just right" books that they have the ability to read with ease. Others organize them by author or by genre without worrying too much about the reading levels; students can choose by interests. There are obviously positives to both types of systems, but one should picture Newcomers or SLIFE. Where are they going to find books? Are they the only students looking for very low reading levels? Are the books obviously for younger children? Are there books in the Newcomers' language? Are there books that represent their culture? Are there books of varying interests that are age-appropriate? We want to make these libraries as inclusive and as encouraging as possible.

Classroom libraries represent something to students: These are the books that they are "allowed" to choose. If the manner in which they are organized is prohibitive to students having a true choice in what they are reading, then the purpose of the library is not met. Also, if the contents of the classroom library are not accessible or diverse, students will not be engaged; rather, reading will be a chore.

We should also be certain to give our students access to different online sites with varieties of electronic books. There are many people who feel that it is "better" or "more authentic" for students to read actual books. However, my position is to encourage reading in whatever form the students prefer. The more books to which they have access, the more likely they may be to find something that sparks their interest or to which they can make a connection!

The key to cultural competence is authenticity. The inclusion of diversity cannot be forced and must be seamless. And, yes, children genuinely can feel if we are authentic or sincere. We have an opportunity—really, the responsibility—to broaden the scope of the perspectives of all students of different cultures.

For a checklist for criteria for choosing quality literature for multilingual learners and tips for working with MLs in small groups, please see the appendix.

5

LEVERAGING NATIVE LANGUAGE

Children's greatest resources in learning are their schema and their confidence. Let's utilize what students already know to help them learn and access what they don't know...yet.

Reflection questions:

- How do you feel when people are speaking with one another in a language that you do not understand?
- What does "accessibility" in the classroom mean for your students?

"Speak English!"

I have heard some well-meaning teachers and administrators admonish students in the hallways and cafeterias when they are speaking in their primary language with their peers. Although I cringe when I hear it, I choose to assume there is a positive intent behind it. Many people feel that complete immersion in school in the target language will help accelerate its acquisition. They figure that these students speak enough Spanish at home. Absolutely not. This is where we have a discussion about the difference between *intent* and *impact*; what is our intention versus the actual result of our actions?

The primary languages of our students must be valued and accepted in our school communities. Languages and cultures are critical parts of our identity. ***"Don't be ashamed you can't speak English yet. You can still learn a lot in school before you can"***—translated from a student. When one tells a student that they cannot speak their language in our school, we send the message that their language is not worthwhile or as important as English. The student feels like an outsider looking into the English-speaking world. We certainly do not want anyone to think that, unless they speak English, they have nothing of value to say.

Speaking a language that is not one's primary language can be mentally and physically exhausting. Sometimes just to unwind a bit by talking in one's primary language can help alleviate the stress of "being on" all day. Although using the target language is the goal, constantly translating in one's head and wondering if they are using the correct words can cause students to feel tired and frustrated. If they are not able to communicate well in the target language yet, it may be a relief to be able to speak and understand while using their primary language without a struggle.

Other students, particularly in the upper grades, have such self-consciousness about speaking in English that they remain quiet. Obviously, we strive to build our students up and boost their self-confidence, but we have to remember that children (and adults!) develop language at their own pace. As one gets more confidence and trust that attempts at language will be supported, they will begin to take risks in producing it.

Speaking their primary language may also boost feelings of belonging and connectivity to a group if there are others (students or adults) who share that language. ***"Together we can learn everything"***—translated. Instead of being an outsider who does not know the language of the group, they can fully communicate in their primary language. They may feel that they have more they are able to contribute if they are able to do so in their dominant language. Nadia is an ESL teacher whose native language is Bulgarian; however, she has shared that she values the dominant language of her students so much that she is learning Spanish in her free time. She says it is to better relate to them and to help them learn literary concepts (such as elements of a story) or phonics (among other skills) using skills they already have in their dominant language. Not only does this help Nadia connect with her students and help make content accessible for them, but the students love witnessing her own language-learning journey as well. (*If she can put the effort in and not be afraid to make mistakes, maybe I can do the same??*)

When our students are in class and have gotten to the point at which they have enough English for communication, there are times in which gently encouraging them that English is their target language is acceptable. If students are working in collaborative groups within the classroom, a gentle reminder from the teacher may be appropriate in certain circumstances. At this point, the students are more comfortable with social and academic language in English and simply may have forgotten which language they are using when speaking—as funny as that sounds! However, even these students may prefer to speak their primary language in the hallways and cafeteria, and this must be supported and respected by all staff members. The sound of different languages in the school—particularly in the common areas—is a clear indicator of how inclusive the community is for all.

Primary or dominant language support

If available, use of the primary language of Newcomers can engage them in a way that helps them academically, emotionally and socially. This could be in any of the four domains of language (listening, speaking, reading or writing) and can help build a bridge of communication in terms of content understanding. But there are several things to consider when translating.

Translating can be considered to be a scaffold that helps provide the supports that students may need to engage in the content area. Much like all scaffolds, using the primary language must be done only to the extent that the student needs that support without providing more support than the student needs. With that being said, the goal is to provide only the amount that students need for understanding. As students' English proficiency increases, the scaffolds decrease. To be clear, this is not lowering standards for acquisition of the target language; rather this is giving access to the content being taught while activating prior schema.

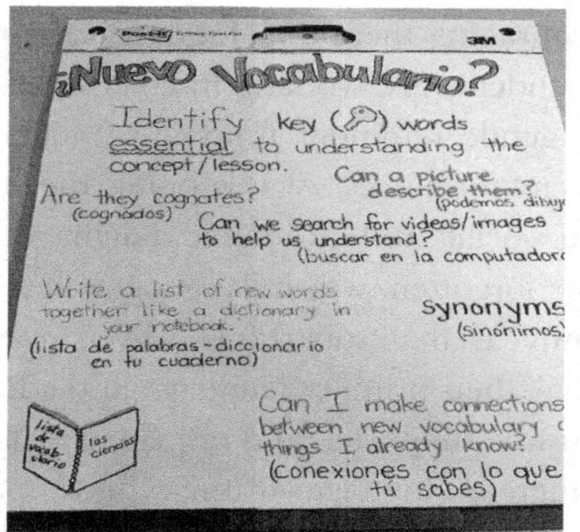

Most times, entire documents or presentations do not need to be translated. When a student is brand-new to our country, we focus on content learning, but also language acquisition. These students should be learning key concepts with vocabulary in both languages. Focusing on cognates within passages or documents is key, as well. If your Newcomers do not learn every single content detail that your native speakers (or even MLs who have more English skills!) do, please do not worry! As long as they are gaining information in the content and being exposed to English, they are learning!

Although we may want to translate everything, some of our students, especially our SLIFE, may not know the complex vocabulary of our content areas *in their native language*, so translating would not meet their needs. Some students also have limited literacy in their native language. Please use visuals and diagrams with basic English to help them understand. We also find that there is an abundance of videos across the content areas that can help students build schema. If these students have some literacy in their primary language, videos with subtitles (in which they hear the English but can read in their primary language) are very effective.

Jessica created this anchor chart to support her Newcomers in learning the months of the year in English. She added the pronunciation in Spanish (all of her students happened to speak Spanish as their dominant language) underneath each month. The visuals that she created to go alongside each month are culturally representative of the month in New Jersey, even though they may not be the case in the students' native countries. So, this anchor chart covers many bases: pronunciation leveraging dominant language, comprehensible input in the target language with visuals to support, and also cultural connections to the climate or celebrations of the place where the students are learning.

Providing abbreviated translated notes with only basic concepts of lessons can help provide schema for students. Avoid passages or notes that are very heavy on language with few visuals. Having scaffolding notes as a resource while listening to comprehensible input during class can help students make connections between their primary language and English.

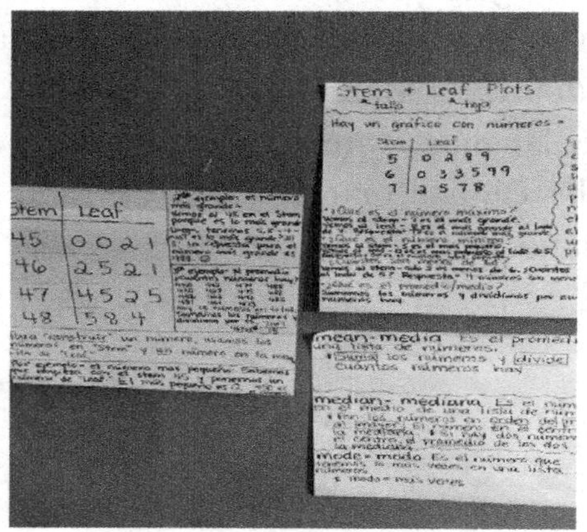

Allowing students to use technology such as Google Translate or hand-held translators to translate key vocabulary for themselves is a great way to make them a stakeholder in their own learning. They can also use Google images if that helps. When students understand their content and language objectives for an assignment, they may work independently using various resources to achieve those goals.

Creating anchor charts or visuals as a reference for common question words or instructions in the native language is a powerful way to engage students in utilizing resources as they need them. Kara creates all anchor charts in her language arts classroom in the languages of the students in her classroom, especially ones that are to be used as reference guides during independent work or reading. These types of visuals within the classroom can help students become more confident in the content and independent as they have the same visual cues as their English-speaking peers.

Language output in writing can be differentiated. If students write entirely in their dominant language, they can go back and translate keywords into English to help demonstrate to you that they understand concepts. Translanguaging is an extremely valid and valuable form of language use and can help build confidence and schema in both languages. According to Cummins (2018), insisting that students keep their languages separate while speaking or writing language is NOT productive for communication. Allowing them to leverage their knowledge in both languages—especially when using academic language—can provide students with opportunities to learn language and content at the same time.

Assigning bilingual "peer buddies" is a great strategy, but with a few cautions. Make sure your buddies are strong students so they do not fall behind in their own work. Buddies also must be compassionate and patient (perhaps a former ML?). Changing up buddies often will allow our Newcomers to form connections with many students and also relieve some of the possible "stress" on peer buddies. However, students should not be assigned to "translate" for our Newcomers; it really is the responsibility of the educational staff to ensure that all students' educational and linguistic needs are being met. If students clarify or are working in collaborative groups together, then the bilingual buddies are in the situation in which the dominant language can be used for supporting the Newcomers.

Remember that the native language is a great tool to use, but exposure to English is key! Be patient and be encouraging—we are cultivating bilingual adults!

Reflection discussion:

Reflection 1: Many people report feeling uncomfortable when surrounded by people speaking a language that they do not understand. People often feel that people are talking about them or that they are saying something they wouldn't like. They may feel that the use of another language is a deliberate way to exclude someone else. These perceptions may lead to feeling resentful when they are around others who are speaking a different language.

Well. People need to get over it. Maybe someone is talking about them. Maybe they are not. (They probably aren't; I always find it funny how people think everyone else is thinking about them all the time.) Either way, people (including children) have the right to speak in the language of their choosing when conversing with people.

Our Newcomers come to us with so many challenges already that they do not need to add resentment of people who perceive that they are speaking unkindly when speaking in their dominant language. Teachers sometimes let their own insecurities prevent them from seeing the necessity of these students to speak in their dominant language, especially when speaking informally with a peer. As educators, we must always consider the point of view of our students and model what is appropriate and respectful behavior. Please do not teach your other students to behave negatively when others are speaking in different languages.

When students feel valued and know that their dominant language is accepted, there may be less of an environment in which students "use" their language to speak poorly about others. That resentment just won't be there...if it even ever was.

Reflection 2: Although at this point our MLs are not covered by specific laws in terms of language for instructional practice or teacher-to-student ratios as our students with special education classifications are, we can agree that *accessibility* is key for these students—whatever it looks like. What does it mean to make content and language accessible for these students?

When I first began teaching, my ESL students were not engaged in their content-area classes. They were given tasks (such as puzzles) to keep them busy while other children were involved in the learning. They literally took up space in the classes and the teachers may not have even known if they spoke English at all. This may be an extreme situation—that was hopefully much more common all those years ago than it is now—but I think it paints a pretty clear picture of what lack of accessibility can be. It is the absolute right of all students to have access to the same grade-level material as their peers, even if it sometimes looks different to ensure understanding.

However, accessibility is many things, with only some of them directly connected to instruction. Following are some questions to consider when examining student accessibility.

Are language and vocabulary explicitly taught in content areas? Do teachers utilize visuals, graphic organizers, and charts to help students make connections to key words? Are all teachers considered to be English language teachers, even if they teach math, science, or social studies?
Are students mainstreamed into general education classes or are they segregated throughout the day? Within those classes, are they interspersed within the class or are they their own little group in a corner?
Do all teachers share responsibility of serving MLs in their class or do they "belong" to the ESL teacher? If there is more than one teacher in the room, do they co-teach? Or is the ESL teacher viewed as an assistant?
Is technology available to students to use as necessary for translations? Can technology be used for visuals, videos, or other ways to provide opportunities for students to engage with the content? On the other hand, is technology used as a substitute for real human interaction?
Are students given the opportunity to participate in the activities of the class? Or are they "engaged" in other assignments?
Is there communication with the students' families? Does this communication only involve the ESL staff or do others take that initiative too?
Are communications to the students' homes translated as needed? Are lunch menus or report card comments translated? Are students' families supported if applying for free or reduced lunch? If students have IEPs or 504 Plans, are these documents translated?
Are Newcomers or MLs represented among the school's clubs, teams, and student leadership? Are ESL teachers represented among school leadership as well?
Is the home language of the students respected and do students feel that it is valued? Is translanguaging supported or encouraged when appropriate?
Does the classroom and district library literature represent the student population's languages and cultures?

To be clear, there is more to these students than their dominant language. By respecting and including their knowledge of their dominant language, we can connect with them in positive ways that include all of the wonderful aspects of themselves: their personalities, their learning styles, their cultures, their families, and the list goes on. These students have much to contribute to the school community and should be represented across the campus.

For a list of tips to share with your colleagues about engaging MLs, please see the appendix.

6

PROVIDING SUPPORT IN COMPREHENSIBLE ENGLISH

Providing opportunities for MLs to understand and interact in English in a way that is comprehensible and accessible to them is truly giving the gift of a new language.

Reflection questions:

- In addition to language, what are some challenges that MLs and their families experience?
- How can these challenges of MLs be viewed from an asset-based perspective?

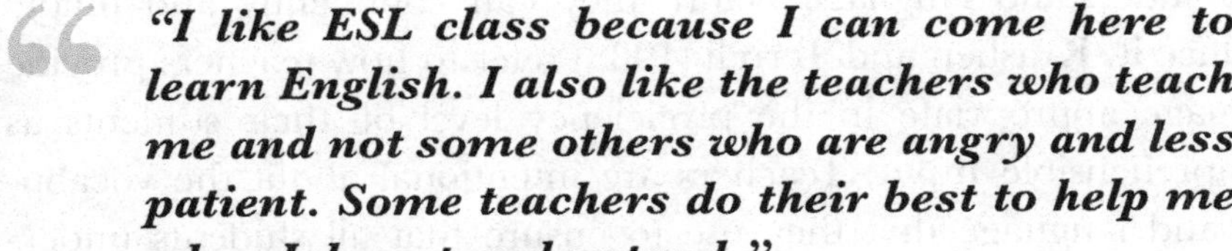

"I like ESL class because I can come here to learn English. I also like the teachers who teach me and not some others who are angry and less patient. Some teachers do their best to help me when I do not understand."

COLOs

I have yet to meet a teacher who adores doing lesson plans. With this being said, they are a necessary evil sometimes, especially the sections that specify objectives, learning targets and evaluations. These parts of the plan keep us "intentional" with our activities and how students will be assessed in each lesson. This intentionality reminds us that the minutes we have in class with our students are valuable and we must use that time as wisely as possible.

Teachers of MLs—both as ESL teachers and general education teachers—take the role of language and content teachers and it is best practice to provide objectives for both (COLOs). The content objective focuses on the concepts being learned (and measured) having to do with the material of the lesson. The language objective describes the type of language use that will be in focus to support the content objective. Language objectives concern the four domains of language: speaking, listening, reading and writing.

<u>Content objective</u>: Students will analyze the points of view of three different perspectives of the Spanish colonization of the Americas.

<u>Language objectives</u>: Students will *listen* to a book and watch a video in the target language about the Spanish colonization of the Americas. Students will *collaborate* in groups to *complete* sentence stems about Columbus' arrival and *defend* their choice of verb.

Acquisition through language *input* usually develops first with MLs, as they understand language before they can confidently and fluidly produce it. Krashen and Terrell (1983) refer to how teachers provide language appropriate to the proficiency level of their students as Comprehensible Input. Teachers are intentional about the vocabulary and language that they use to ensure that all students understand. Content vocabulary is clarified, speaking rate is at a pace that is easily understood, and there are frequent checks for understanding. Also, input does not necessarily only refer to spoken language; input may include visual input as well as written supports to scaffold language comprehension.

Language *output* may develop in ways as individual to the student. Sometimes students are reluctant to speak in the target language for fear of mistakes, but they are actively and productively acquiring language all the time. Krashen and Terrell (1983) refer to this as the "Silent Period," which can last for different amounts of time in different learners. Teachers must be aware of this period and not assume that their students have a disability that prevents them from speaking in the target language. As students are beginning to increase language output, teachers can focus on language output at the single word level first, then moving to sentences and finally, paragraphs or essays.

COLOs are not just for MLs, but rather just good practice for teachers of all students. Content-area teachers have the responsibility to include language work in their classes, as all students are continually learning the complex academic language in content areas as they move through the grades. Teachers cannot assume that students already know this language, regardless of their target language proficiency. In other words, all students are language learners in these classes, not just the MLs.

Building and activating schema

"Frontloading" vocabulary is effective for activating schema. Before a lesson, unit, or chapter, teachers highlight specific vocabulary words that are key to understanding the upcoming information. I recommend that the teacher choose 5-6 keywords or phrases to highlight to keep the list manageable. Using a variety of modalities, students work with vocabulary before encountering the words in the lesson/chapter. This can help build their schema and background knowledge of the topic before they tackle the rest of the content.

Don't assume students know about things that happened in American or world history or are aware of current events. Often teachers say that a concept is a review because it was covered in the curriculum of a previous grade; however, Newcomers were not students in the school at that time and it probably is not a review for them. Academically, the most dangerous thing a teacher can say: "As I'm sure you've learned in the past..." ***"I wish that my teacher knew that I don't know much of history and science because I never learn it. They always give me E's when I don't answer a question or when I don't do the work they give me but I do not know how."*** If there are concepts that are integral to new lessons/skills/readings that may be covered in previous curricula, please consider opportunities to make these connections for students who may not have learned this information.

When introducing a concept that may be new for Newcomers, effective practice includes printing out or showing students pictures of concepts or people about which you are teaching with keywords for them to research on the internet for more information. The visuals help them make the connections between the vocabulary and concepts with the pictures and will help build their schema.

When providing notes or background, information with simpler English with only key information and images is helpful. If you are lecturing or providing information to the whole group, please give information in chunks with short activities in between so Newcomers can process and internalize the content and language. Providing too much language at one time is overwhelming for many of our students.

Sources such as Newsela or Epic may have passages about topics in different curricula written on varied reading levels or in different languages and can provide an option for all students to work on the same objectives on different levels. If students cannot read even lower levels in English, identify keywords for them to translate themselves. With enough keywords, ask them to write summaries about what they think is going on in the passage.

"Survival English"

When students arrive from other countries (or school districts!), sometimes teachers view them as a blank slate just waiting to be "filled" with information. We are so passionate about what we teach that we just cannot wait to share all we know with our students. However, in the first weeks and months that our Newcomers are here, we must be judicious with what English we immediately focus on. ***"I want the ESL teachers to teach me words that will help me understand what the teachers say in other classes. I want to understand but sometimes they don't explain things to me"***—translated.

We want to make our students independent and empowered as quickly as possible, and our focus on teaching them the language that helps them communicate their needs and connect with other students and teachers first is crucial. If the Newcomers are younger, we find that they will be learning this vocabulary right along with their classmates as Dual Language Learners (DLLs). However, when older Newcomers arrive, there must be explicit instruction in vocabulary that they can put to use immediately. This will show them that they have the ability to use the target language in a way that may not be perfect, but in which they can communicate with others.

Some of the topics that are appropriate for Newcomers to learn in English right away may include:

Students must immediately know the vocabulary for expressing their name, grade, and teacher. I always practice this information immediately with students and give them a visual in their notebook/agenda book that indicates who they are and that they are an ESL student. If there are situations in which students are being addressed or questioned by staff who don't know that they may not understand the language, this should be the way they can communicate that they are not being disrespectful or not listening.
Self-advocacy vocabulary such as asking for the restroom, the nurse, or a drink during class is critical from day one. Also, "I need help" or "I don't understand" are useful to know how to express.
Expressing their address and phone number and understanding the language used when this information is being requested is important. This may not be crucial in school, but depending upon their age, this may be something that they need in the community.
Basic greetings are a formulaic and low-stress way that students can get used to producing the target language in a way that doesn't require much in response. Students can interact with others in socially appropriate ways ("Hi, how are you?" "Fine, thank you. You?") while gaining confidence to speak more after those interactions are successful. Some of my most enjoyable times with Newcomers is introducing them to phrases to use with peers, such as "What's up?"
Understanding of question words (Who? What?) is also a way to help students recognize what teachers and others may be asking. This can also help them ask simple questions, even if they begin with the question word and motion the rest.
Basic direction words that students will encounter: Draw, list, write, cut, glue, color, underline, match… If students understand these key words, they will be able to start their assignments more independently and with more confidence.

Content-area language

There are so many things that seem to us so urgent that our Newcomers learn immediately. Each content area has its own "survival vocabulary" that students need to quickly learn upon which to build other concepts. This is where multilingual word walls or anchor charts come into play. Math teachers can create anchor charts shaped into the different operations (addition would look like a plus, subtraction a minus, etc) with clue words inside each. Science teachers can have anchor charts that show laboratory vocabulary or the layers of the earth in the languages represented in the class. Students do not necessarily have to learn those words right away, but they should have them easily accessible to them in the class in which they will need them. A combination of symbols, visuals, and vocabulary can be an excellent way to help students connect the concept with the target language.

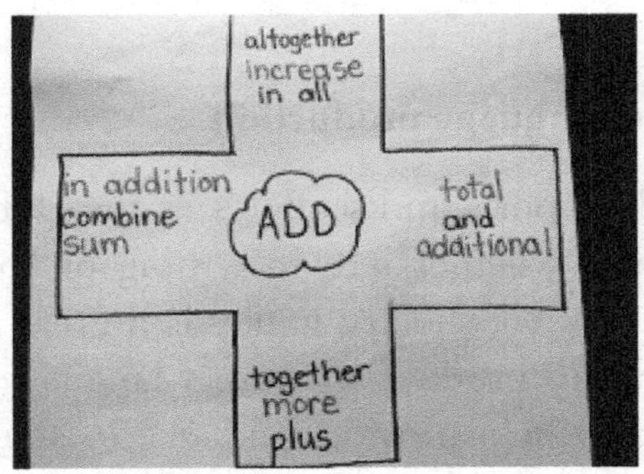

According to the work of Cummins (2000), as students learn the different types of proficiencies in language acquisition (BICS/CALP), they go through different processes to acquire them. BICS (Basic Interpersonal Communication Skills) is acquired through more of an authentic, social context, much like the acquisition of first language skills as a young child. Repetition, learning through interactions with others, and putting names and words to one's world are all the ways that one learns basic parts of language. As students understand and produce more of the social language needed to interact with peers and adults, they build confidence that can help them tackle more difficult language.

CALP (Cognitive Academic Language Proficiency) includes the use of language that is more academic in nature than the social language described above. Academic language, however, can be acquired in a number of different ways. Teachers must be certain to provide opportunities in all four language domains (listening, speaking, reading, writing) when introducing new language in academic concepts. ***"I want most to understand what math says. I know there***

is a lot to learn. I have to understand the words first"—translated. This is where the COLOs and attention to teaching academic vocabulary come into focus. In order to best understand the concepts, all students must have explicit instruction on the academic vocabulary associated with the lesson.

Opportunities for language production

Newcomers need supports and scaffolds as they attempt to produce the target language, whether it is in writing or speaking out loud. Keeping a list of key vocabulary handy is a great way to empower students to attempt to produce the target language. Sentence stems and frames can also help provide guidance to students as they are producing more complex language.

Providing sentence frames is a scaffold in assisting students in writing in the target language and providing a framework for your expectations for the assignment. Sentence frames provide language exposure for students to leverage in order to build their knowledge of vocabulary, syntax, and analysis of context clues. The support provides a framework of a sentence with blanks in which students can place the target vocabulary. This can be part of the Writing Workshop or can be a way to engage in new vocabulary. Visuals and word banks are useful when necessary, but be sure to only provide the scaffolds that students need. This can also be how work is differentiated for different levels of proficiency.

The characters' names are ___________ and ___________.
The setting is ___________ ( ) and  ___________ ( ). They are important because ______________________________.
The conflict is between the ________________ and the colonists.
_______ + _______ =

This may look like a Cloze writing activity, but there are some differences. With sentence frames, there may be a "correct" answer or there may be flexibility with the answers if they make sense. They may be used in terms of information from a story, retelling an event, or even as an assessment following a lesson. Other options include writing that is more individualized to the student, such as information about the student's own lives or experiences. The key is to keep the language work connected to lessons or reading and from random language use in isolation.

Sentence stems are useful ways to set students up for writing in the target language. These may be modeling ways to begin writing prompts and, again, should be connected to what students are doing. They can also be used across the content area. These are used as students are becoming more comfortable with producing the language but need some guidance.

My opinion about the character is....
What I liked best about the class trip was...
I wonder...
When I put the magnet on the toaster...

Sentence stems can be used as journal topics, answers to open-ended content questions, or in free writing. There is flexibility in the language that students can add to these stems and they are models of ways to use the language. Transition words can also be parts of sentence stems, both exposing students to writing conventions and vocabulary associated with the topic. Sentence stems that can be useful in different situations are most effective and students can gain confidence as they become more comfortable with those phrases.

Sentence stems can also be effective when students are speaking the language. When I give MLs the opportunity to speak in the target language, I often give them the topic ahead of time and let them prepare themselves and understand the vocabulary. This allows them time to produce the vocabulary (sometimes even taking notes or writing out sentences!) and diminishes the stress and nerves of not having a chance to prepare themselves. I think it is very important to recognize that it's acceptable for students to acknowledge that they need more time to process and produce language.

Sometimes the daunting part about producing language is getting started. Both of these techniques can provide some structure and support that can stimulate language use, as well as boosting confidence as students are interacting with the target language.

Krashen's low affective filter

Krashen and Terrell (1983) discuss how the environment of the class (and I would add hallways, cafeteria, offices of the school) can affect the way students acquire language. If the environment is an emotionally safe place for learners to take risks in producing language, they will attempt to speak in the target language. Conversely, if the students feel that their attempts at speaking in the target language will be situations in which they will be ridiculed or constantly corrected, they will not be willing to take that risk.

How do teachers and admin establish and maintain a low affective filter in the classroom (and other areas in the school)?

On Day 1, the classroom and school must be established as a supportive environment. No one is in competition, and no one gets a prize for pointing out others' shortcomings. It's a family and we cheer for and support one another.
Teachers must take care when they are "cold calling" on students or asking them to read aloud to the class. I always attempt to make eye contact with students who I think may be uncertain about participating to see if they look petrified or willing to try. I also allow students to say "Pass" if they are uncomfortable with speaking in front of the class. Of course, knowing your students is key here. Some may need some encouragement and others may still be in a silent period.
Similarly, avoid "Round Robin" reading, when the students read aloud by where they are seated in the room. It's outdated and creates an environment filled with anxiety for many students. Students also are often counting paragraphs or sentences to practice in their heads what they are going to be required to read aloud—while missing key information.
If participation out loud is desired, give students the opportunity to write or prepare their response. Allyssa uses Readers' Theater in her Social Studies class that has parts with different levels of challenge. She assigns the parts to MLs ahead of time and gives them plenty of opportunities to practice. During the read-through, they are nervous but so excited to be ready to participate! The other students in the class were so happy that the MLs in the class were reading out loud and in English that they were telling the rest of their teachers about it all day. This type of classroom environment creates stakeholders in all students' successes.
Teacher read-alouds are fantastic for creating a literacy—and language-rich classroom environment in which students are comfortable. When teachers read out loud to students, there is an opportunity for students to relax and enjoy listening to quality literature. This literature may be beyond their language level or literacy level, but hearing the words, seeing the pictures (if applicable), and having positive experiences with reading are key. Teachers can model strategies and discuss higher-level thinking as a class. Please note that your middle and high school students are not too old to benefit from this; I have even recommended read-alouds in literacy classes at the community college level;
Collaborative learning groups must be intentionally formed with plenty of support for MLs. If there are bilingual students who share language with the MLs, that's helpful...but it's not a game-changer if there's not. Create stakeholders for Newcomers' success by creating opportunities for helpful students to work together with the Newcomers.

Mistakes:

Have you ever experienced a class "catching" the teacher in a mistake? This can be either a mortifying experience for the teacher or a positive teachable moment for all involved. One of the lessons that I learned later in my career is that mistakes are nothing of which to be ashamed. Certainly, I'm not perfect and it would be too exhausting to pretend I am. But, that feeling comes with having confidence in yourself—and it's possible that your students do not yet feel that way yet. Modeling respect in terms of correcting mistakes and owning your own is such an important skill to share with your students. But, the key is to embed this in your classroom culture.

On the first day, I talk about mistakes: how I make them, students make them, and they are part of learning. No one is permitted to correct another student except the teacher—and only then in a supportive way. Laughing or shouting out corrections is not tolerated. If a teacher makes a mistake, students certainly can respectfully identify the mistake in the spirit of learning. Hopefully, the teacher and class can have a good laugh about the mistake and move on. If the focus on mistakes (our own and others') is to support learning, there is no joy in pointing out the errors of others. The tone of the class is "I've got you!" rather than "Gotcha!"

Should teachers focus on correcting all errors? This is a personal choice and influences your classroom climate. When students are reading aloud or speaking, I only choose to correct the mistakes that I feel are absolutely essential to the objective of the lesson or the story. Other mistakes—for which the content is still understandable—are fine to let go. You don't want your students to feel that every word they say is going to be corrected; no one will want to take a chance and participate. I also choose three pieces of constructive, actionable feedback upon which to focus when grading writing pieces, rather than giving back a paper that is torn apart with corrections. Students may focus more on learning from their mistakes if they aren't presented with too many to consider. Again, if students know that they can take risks and still be supported, they will be more likely to try to go out of their comfort zone.

Another perspective on mistakes is: "If I let them go, how will students learn?" This is certainly valid and depends on your teaching style, content area, and students in your class. Correcting mistakes is often connected to having high expectations for students and the desire to ensure they learn as much as possible. If students are making mistakes with certain parts of grammar or specific vocabulary, teacher modeling is particularly effective in giving students the opportunity to hear the correct way of expressing the language. My suggestion is to reflect on what approach (or combination of approaches) would most benefit your students—what is good for kids is always the right way to do things.

Remember, communication is key. As students are testing the waters with speaking in English, any utterances that are understandable are celebrated, no matter the errors. As students are improving and their confidence is stronger, their mistakes can be turned into teachable moments—just not to the point that they shut down because everything they say is corrected.

Reflection discussion:

Reflection 1: Language is the first and perhaps most obvious challenge that teachers may encounter when working with Newcomers. Through the four domains of language (listening, speaking, reading, writing), teachers communicate with students and learn about them and their lives. When students have little prior experience with the language of the classroom or teacher, this may seem insurmountable. ***"I think the teacher is angry with me when I don't understand"***—translated. From the perspective of the student, this can be frustrating, frightening, and intimidating.

Whether or not students are SLIFE, they must be placed upon arrival in the grade that is most appropriate to their age. While this is done with social and emotional health in mind, it also may put students in a position in which they are not set up for success without intense academic intervention. We know how much the content of each grade builds on the previous concepts that students learned in prior grades. When Newcomers arrive who have missed significant time in education, it can sometimes feel to them that they have little chance for success.

In addition to academic challenges, Newcomers may be leaving their home country under less-than-ideal circumstances. Family may be left behind, as is everything they have ever known. There may be trauma or sadness that surrounds this enormous life change, and some students may still be dealing with these emotions.

Navigating a new country with different systems is difficult for anyone, let alone families who may not know the language. Understanding the system of money, healthcare, their rights as a tenant (if applicable), school schedules, employment, different foods, navigating transportation, and the norms attached to all these things are very challenging to grasp for many people.

When needing help, they may encounter neighbors or townspeople with preconceived notions about people in their situation. There are sometimes two cultures in a town: the one people admit and embrace in public and the one that shows up in situations in which people feel comfortable enough to show their true feelings. ***"I'm going to talk to the principal this summer. My son has 'put his time in' with those kids*** [MLs] ***in his class and he will not be with them again next year."*** These parents may be on the PTA, the school board, or other groups of power within the school community. If a parent knows that their child is part of a group that is marginalized in school is difficult; when the child knows it, it's heartbreaking.

Reflection 2: Viewing all students from an asset-based perspective is crucial, but not natural to everyone to do all the time. It's so easy to get caught up in one's challenges that we forget to focus on the positive. The following are some of the things upon which teachers may focus when meeting a Newcomer or SLIFE and some other ways to look at them. Some may be changes in perspective and some may be ways that we as educators can support these children and their families.

This child doesn't speak a word of English. This child is a future bilingual. As educators, we must think about the Power of

YET. The child may not have a grasp of the English language YET. But it will happen. And multilingualism is such an asset for any individual.

This student missed a ton of school. What am I supposed to do with them in fourth grade? This child may have missed years or had inconsistent schooling. However, this does not mean that there is nothing we can do for them. With appropriate support and intervention if necessary, we can certainly help them progress. Key to understand is that his learning may temporarily not look like the learning of other age-similar peers. They may have to learn concepts that are below grade level at first. However, if we concentrate on assessing what they are learning (rather than what they do not know), with the right supports, they will show progress.

This student doesn't do homework. As frustrating as it is for teachers when students do not do homework, we must think sometimes about the reason behind the behavior. Does the student work after school? Does the student have to care for siblings? Does the student have any support or anyone to help them at home if they don't understand? Is homework something that the student is able to complete independently? Are they so exhausted mentally and physically from trying to get through the school day in two languages that they can't do it? It's crucial that teachers do not assume that they do not want to learn or aren't motivated if they don't complete homework. It may be a symptom of another situation entirely. And students who have these types of responsibilities in their family and outside of school are possibly helping their family stay afloat—which is definitely an asset.

They can't read in their own language, so they'll never read in English. Research shows that language learners who have literacy in their dominant language are able to transfer those skills into learning how to read in the target language. These students show strengths in literacy in both languages. However, if students do not have literacy in their dominant language, that does not mean that they are unable or unwilling to learn to read in either language. Targeted instruction is needed to help establish those sound-symbol-word relationships that such students must learn. Once this is understood, literacy can be developed in both languages. Again, what appears at this moment to be an obstacle will be a building block towards cultivating a multilingual adult!

I know they can understand me. They don't listen. Sometimes the whirlwind of English can be overwhelming for MLs and they tire from processing in two languages all day. As difficult as it is to understand, sometimes tuning people out is simply a "self-care" mechanism. So, from an assets-based perspective, this student is possibly working so hard just trying to keep up that they may have to take a break and tune out. Gently reminding them to focus again may be all they need to listen carefully again. The most important thing to remember is that the responsibility for comprehensible input is with the teacher. If the student cannot understand (or at least get an idea) of what is going on, the teacher must reflect upon how to present things differently.

I think this student just cannot learn. ALL students can learn. And these children HAVE learned, throughout their entire lives. They may have learned in school. They may have learned on their family's farm. They may have learned in church. They definitely learned an immeasurable amount while on their trip to a new country. They definitely learned a lot upon their arrival and getting settled. They definitely learned when they first showed up at a new school and every single moment since. Just because their lifelong learning doesn't look like some people's perception of what learning should be, that doesn't mean that they haven't learned—and possibly have learned more than many of us who now teach them!

These parents never come to conferences. They just don't care. Parents may not come to conferences or meetings at the school for a variety of reasons, as we have discussed. However, these parents may be working so very hard for the benefit of their families. These children see a family unit who is going quite literally to the ends of the earth for one another. Similarly, although these parents care very much, they may not understand the importance (or even received notice!) of these meetings with the teachers. Schools in other countries may not have the tradition of these conferences and parents may feel that the teachers have things under control. Teachers reaching out to these parents in supportive ways will help engage them in ways that are positive.

This student doesn't even know math. Isn't that a universal language? Math is not a universal language, no matter how it appears. Even if our Newcomers come from a country that uses a similar numerical system as in their new country (some do and some do not), there are still issues with the transfer. Word problems and math vocabulary are obvious challenges for these students, but also the formation of numbers may be different, too. On a positive note, the different ways that these students have experienced math may help lead to a deeper understanding of the concepts as they learn more.

This student is so poorly behaved in school. Whether or not our Newcomers have had much experience in a "traditional" school setting, it may not have many similarities to schools in their new country. They may not know the concept of "raising your hand" or asking to be excused when leaving the room. Collaborative learning may be a foreign concept to them. When introducing students to the norms and rules of a school that may be completely different from what they have experienced, one must be sure to be patient and consistent. With that being said, as frustrating as it is to have a student who does not follow the rules as the others do, simply engaging them in the class will go a long way in remedying that.

I can't even call his parents because they don't speak English. What can teachers who do not speak the home language of these students do? Reaching out in different ways to communicate with the parents is crucial, especially when they are not able to come into the school. If there is no one in the school who speaks the dominant language of the student, then the communication may have to be in writing, translated through an app or website. But, language differences should never be used as an excuse not to communicate (both positively and with concerns) with a parent. Those parents—and that child—deserve it just as much as everyone else does.

If we view all of our students as an integral and important part of our class and school family, then we focus on the positives that everyone brings to the table. This is particularly helpful to remind ourselves and our colleagues when all we see are the challenges.

For more samples of sentence stems and sentence frames, please find them in the appendix. A sample lesson plan with COLOs included in the appendix as well.

7

PLAYING "CATCH UP"

All students, even SLIFE, have the capacity to learn. It is up to their teachers to provide the opportunity, support, and patience to help them.

Reflection questions:

- What is the role of literacy when working with Newcomers and SLIFE?
- Should SLIFE be referred for special education services?

A "Perfect Storm"

There are so many challenges that all Newcomers must overcome when they first arrive in a school in a new country. Making a monumental life change such as this is an enormous adjustment that often comes with feelings of loss, grief, anxiety, and excitement. Along with not knowing the language to the mix, our

Newcomers may have mountains to climb and rivers to cross (sometimes literally and figuratively!).

Some Newcomers come to our schools with a solid foundation of literacy and education in their native country in their primary language. These students can build on their language and literacy that has already been developed in their primary language to transfer skills to acquire the target language in their new country. Cognates, knowledge of sign-sound relationships, and understanding of literacy strategies in their primary language all support these students as they begin their journey in the target language.

Some parents may be supportive of education and have read to their children daily in their native language. Constant conversation in forms of "mother-ese" engage children in the use of vocabulary from the time they are born to when they are developing literacy. Reading together for these families is a loving, positive experience, and children associate books with cuddles and attention from loved ones. Other parents may have little background in literacy and possibly never experienced an adult reading to or interacting with themselves in this type of way. These parents may also be living lives that do not permit them this luxury of interacting with their children in this way; long hours at work, the stress of keeping the family afloat, large families, and oppressive responsibilities are very real reasons why some parents cannot actively support early literacy and language development. Access to books in the home for them is another real challenge. Many families may fall somewhere in between these examples.

Another factor in vocabulary development is affected by the environment in which some families live when they arrive in their new country. We have found that some entire families live in a single room in a house. In fear of being evicted if they are too loud, these families may try to keep children quiet rather than encouraging conversation. Families don't want to make any waves or be disruptive to the other tenants. Especially with our younger students, we found that language production is sometimes discouraged so no one will complain about the noise (Shhh!) and possibly get them evicted or in trouble with the landlord. This is yet another way that SES may have a very real effect on language and literacy development.

Additionally, in some cultures, children should be "seen and not heard." In these families, children are exposed to conversations among adults, but often receive directions or short commands with limited vocabulary and few opportunities to express language in the home. Obviously, there is no judgment about these cultures, but teachers can very intentionally produce language and provide opportunities for language production in class.

These variables, according to Logan (2019), at Ohio State University, may contribute to a "million-word gap" before age 5 between children whose parents read and intentionally converse daily with their young children and children of parents who do not habitually do this. Logan's study focused on children in their native language; some of our MLs are now trying to build on this deficit to acquire a second language. For these children, literacy and vocabulary development in school is critical. Teachers can certainly not take the place of parents, but we do have the amazing responsibility to meet children wherever they are and meet their needs.

In addition to language and literacy "storms," our Newcomers have the daunting task of finding their space in a world that is new and different for them. They may not know school norms or understand why people may be annoyed that they do not know the rules. They may feel isolated or scared in their new communities. They may not know if this school is a place that they will stay or if it is simply a stop in their journey. They may have food insecurity and do not have the strength to go through the mental exhaustion it requires to understand what is happening in school all day. Nothing is "automatic" for these children, as it may be for others.

"What can I do to meet their needs?"

We need to be clear that a child's background as a SLIFE is NOT a prison sentence and should not be treated as such. Also to be noted is that these children do not deserve punishment or stigma attached to their educational background. These students are absolutely capable of learning (and have learned continually over their lives) with access to appropriate intervention and content instruction. Their needs may be different than others in their classes, but the lack of opportunity that these children have experienced does not mean that they do not have a bright academic future.

As our Newcomers come into our schools, we sometimes have to search for information in different places in order to understand their educational backgrounds. We may not even know right away if they are SLIFE or if they have only had a small gap (if any) of schooling as they arrived to us. The Home Language Survey (HLS) and even information from the students themselves will help us start piecing together their unique and wonderful puzzle. To be clear, this "puzzle" is not to figure out what is wrong with our student; rather, this knowledge is power to help us best challenge and support him where needed.

Students (and parents) are usually very honest about their educational past once they understand that they will be supported either way. Once there is a feeling of trust, students and their families will share their concerns and what they feel they need for survival and success.

"He went to school with a shaman in his native country. He did not learn much reading and math."

In addition to academics, there are so many things of which this student's teacher would hopefully be aware.

- What is the purpose of schooling in this student's native country?
- How do the schools measure learning and what do the students learn?
- What are the roles of academics and literacy?
- What is the value of schooling in this community?
- What are the protocols and norms for the schools and how would they compare to this student's new school?
- Is schooling consistent?
- What are this student's feelings about school in general?

Although some designations for students to have SLIFE status require them to have missed 2+ years of schooling, there are some students who do not fit that criteria yet still would benefit from similar supports. For instance, they may have had an education that had a different purpose than ours in the United States. They may have had some experiences with reading and writing in their native language, but not at the level of their agemates in the United States. Math currently may be very difficult for them because they had little background with it in their former school. Thus, although these students did not have any extended periods of time when they were not in school, their schooling may have had very different objectives, and they may not have had access to some academic subjects that we associate with our younger grades.

No matter if the students have had a traditional education or not, I find that often the first class that gives us concern about missed education is math. Teachers appreciate the fact that literacy and language are intertwined, but often feel that math is a universal subject. (It's not necessarily, though! Think of the metric/customary systems and also word problems!) It's not certain that all students who have not missed education will excel in math, but if students are missing key skills in mathematics, this may be a sign these students may be SLIFE.

It's important that these students, whether or not they are SLIFE, have access to grade-level curricula with scaffolds to make them accessible to them. If students are literate in their primary language, one can translate some content and introduce vocabulary in English as needed. If students are SLIFE and do not have strong literacy in their primary language, this is when things get even trickier. Following are some tips and things for teachers to consider when making content accessible for SLIFE:

Introduce key vocabulary first: Frontloading vocabulary is good practice for all students when the vocabulary may be unfamiliar yet essential to understanding the lesson/story/concepts. For SLIFE, however, the vocabulary may be unfamiliar in both the primary and target languages. In this case, visuals can help the student connect the picture to the vocabulary in the target language. Simplified English (phrases, single words) can be translated into the primary language for SLIFE with lower literacy skills and can be added to the visuals. YouTube may have videos spoken in the primary language or with subtitles that can give some background to these students. Verbal recordings of vocabulary can help students gain some background on content. If there is key vocabulary to understand, providing the word in English with a visual is useful.

Cognates: If students speak languages that share similar words with the target language, they can use copies of lower-level passages or texts in English that give information about the content to search for cognates. Sometimes, passages that include visuals alongside key words can help students understand the basic meaning. Students can then write what they think the passage is about based on the words they know. Remember that at the beginning, students may not be getting every detail; that is perfectly acceptable and teachers can work on building background and schema.

Anchor charts: Anchor charts using visuals (or small charts on the students' desks) help remind students of classroom procedures and things to do during independent reading or practice. They are also great ways to remind students of key concepts in the content area.

Word walls: Multilingual word walls are a great reference for students in the content areas. Teachers can put key vocabulary up with visuals and words in students' primary languages. These word walls change with the unit or concept being taught and should be utilized during instruction. (They are word walls, not wallpaper!)

Electronic interactive notebooks: There are a variety of ways that teachers can design these spaces in which students can create their own resources. One idea is to provide one for each unit, and key vocabulary, visuals, and links to videos can all be in one document for easy access for all students. Alternatively, students can use one for a collection of vocabulary that they learn and they can refer back to while producing language.

Passages/reading texts: There are various websites that offer readings on topics in different languages and in varying levels of English. If SLIFE have some literacy in their primary language, this is an option. If not, there are websites that include audios and visuals with small passages. If students are adept at using dictionaries (or at the point at which they can begin to learn), allow them to look up meanings of key vocabulary within a passage (words selected by the teacher as being critical to understanding the passage).

Videos: Many videos about topics in the content area are on the internet and even have translations or subtitles. SLIFE may not be able to read the subtitles quickly or even understand the content vocabulary as it's translated, but the purpose is to build schema for content knowledge.

Building literacy and language through read-alouds

Often as students get older, teachers feel it is less important to read aloud to them. However, reading aloud to students of any age has immeasurable benefits, especially for learners who may be struggling readers. Students do not "age out" of these benefits, no matter their target language proficiency!

Reading aloud exposes students to different types of literature that students may not experience reading themselves. This may include picture books, novels, or any type of literature that engages students, and can certainly be mixed up for variety. If key vocabulary is explicitly taught beforehand, MLs can focus on what they can understand while actively listening. If it is possible to provide students with copies of the literature so they can follow along (or use technology to project to the class), this can also allow them to see and hear the words at the same time, increasing their language input in both domains of language.

Choosing the read-aloud books carefully can give opportunities for teachers to provide *comprehensible input* for MLs (and all students). According to Krashen and Terrell (1983), comprehensible input is the language that teachers and others can use to communicate with language learners; not all words are words that they already understand, but the message is processed and understood by the learner. While reading to the students, teachers can expose them to vocabulary in an authentic context that they may not have heard otherwise. Introducing vocabulary before reading is a valuable activity to help build schema. By stopping, discussing meaning, and modeling strategies, teachers can engage the students in meaningful interactions with literature.

In fact, Krashen (2019) asserts that making the read alouds comprehensible to students who are emergent bilinguals may go beyond reading the words on the pages. Giving background about the story and key vocabulary before reading is effective to help students understand the language and content. Teachers can model strategies to help the students understand unfamiliar words. Providing synonyms or translations when needed can also help make the content comprehensible. Providing visuals or discussing pictures in the book also can engage the students in the literature.

Tina started "First Chapter Fridays" in which she shares the first chapter of a book during class every Friday. Students look forward to it each week, and she chooses from a variety of books to share to appeal to different readers. These are books that aren't necessarily part of her curriculum, but when students have a taste of different genres and types of books, they are intrigued. Again, the attractiveness of the teacher's pick of the book is all these students need to feel that this book is worth their time. The line to read the books following the quick read aloud is long, but students are interested and talking about literature in an engaging way.

Literacy goes beyond reading and writing, and engaging students in storytelling can provide them with language experiences that are invaluable. Feel free to tell stories of your own! They can be based on a picture you find and can engage your students in language like never before. I like to purchase calendars with beautiful pictures when they are on sale each January, laminate them, and use those pictures for many activities in my classroom. Students also love it when you use a picture from your own life about which they can hear a story or talk about what the people may be saying.

For children who may not have had consistent positive literacy time at home, read alouds or storytelling may provide them with enjoyable, relaxing experiences with reading that can help connect reading with joyful feelings. Teachers can choose to "take the floor" with the read-aloud and simply model strategies and thought processes as they read, exposing the students to tone and ways to indicate dialogue without asking students questions while reading. If teachers interact with the students with questions while reading, teachers must be sure not to "cold call" on any one (especially a ML) who is not volunteering to maintain an environment of positivity.

Intervention or no?

To be clear, ESL services for MLs must be viewed as supportive services that provide accessibility to grade-level content rather than as intervention services. It is important to understand that language differences do not mean that students need special education or remediation. I have witnessed many times that students who did not have proficiency in English are considered to be "low" level learners. On the contrary, these students may be gifted in learning and ready for grade-level (or above!) content. At the very least, these students are emergent multilinguals!

SLIFE, however, may need some additional individual support that takes place outside the classroom or with a specialist. If they have not learned key skills associated with the time in school that they have missed, they may need intense instruction or services to help bridge gaps in learning. The teacher must be sure to really consider what is crucial in helping these students learn in order to support their learning grade-level (or closer to grade-level) work. Does it matter if they don't know vocabulary such as farm animals or even (gasp!) how to pronounce the letters of the alphabet in English? Not at this point. However, if they do not understand letter-sound relationships in their primary language or in the target language, that is a critical skill to tackle.

Intervention for MLs or SLIFE doesn't have to mean they are "low" or in need of remedial education. Holding high expectations—yet providing the language and literacy scaffolds to help give accessibility to them—could be the result of intervention. Intervention services are the "bridge" to where these students are going, not where they will remain. These students are working towards grade-level content and standards and sometimes need some more support in a smaller group to achieve them. This "temporary" view of intervention is the difference from Special Education services.

SLIFE or SpEd?

It is really important to understand that our SLIFE may not arrive and be able to work on grade level, even if it is translated into their dominant language. Many of their behaviors and challenges may mirror those of our students with IEPs or learning disabilities. However, we must be certain to distinguish between challenges associated with missed opportunities and true learning disabilities.

My student does not even appear to be able to read in his dominant language even at a basic level. While reading difficulties may certainly be a red flag for learning disabilities sometimes, with SLIFE, we need to take this a couple of steps further.

What schooling did this child receive and what type of school was it?
Are there records from school? Did the child receive supplemental services outside of the classroom?
What does the HLS (Home Language Survey) say about prior school experiences?
Does this child have siblings who also are now in the district? What are those child's teachers finding? Experiences of siblings do not rule out (or suggest) SpEd concerns, but can give us more of an idea of the school/home/academic experiences.
Does this child have emergent literacy book knowledge? This could include the ways to hold a book or turn pages.
How does the child explain own experiences with literacy? Does the child see any success in this arena or does the child only see struggle?
Is there a difference between what this child understands considering the type of language that is presented? Is this academic language or more basic language? We must not assume that these children have been exposed to the same academic language that our students see in previous grades.

My student refuses to speak and does not seem to understand, even when spoken to in his dominant language. Culture shock is a very real thing and some children really struggle with communication while in this phase. There is a documented phase in language acquisition called "The Silent Period" (Krashen & Terrell, 1983) in which learners are absorbing everything from their environment, including verbal and written language, visual cues, non-verbal interactions, and things from their other senses that they find in the environment. Needless to say, there is a lot going on for them, and speaking and processing things in a way they can indicate understanding may not have come yet. People are quick to assume that a child is a "selective mute" or that the child has disabilities, but this is a very real documented phase in language acquisition.

My student does not have number sense or cannot do basic math. Again, we have to determine if this is a result of never having learned these mathematical concepts or if there is a disability in this area. Assessments to see what the child CAN do in math will tell us a lot, and then we can take it from there in terms of seeing what the child can learn. Can the child count things (either in person or on a screen) to represent addition and subtraction? Can the child count with fingers to add or subtract? Does the child understand that some numbers hold a higher value than others? (At this point, avoiding word problems would be beneficial, as we can isolate growth in mathematics without the influence of reading/literacy complicating things.) Once you have determined the child's level in math skills, you can then give the child targeted, individualized interventions on this level and keep data about the progress. Over time, this will tell us if there is a real difficulty in this area or if this child lacked the opportunity to learn these skills and concepts.

He doesn't even know math. Isn't that a universal language? Math is not a universal language, no matter how it appears. Even if our Newcomers come from a country that uses a similar numerical system as in their new country (some do and some do not), there are still issues with the transfer. Word problems and math vocabulary are obvious challenges for these students, but also the formation of numbers may be different, too. Additionally, the use of commas and periods within numbers is different from the US in many countries. On a positive note, the different ways that these students have experienced math may help lead to a deeper understanding of the concepts as they learn more.

I suspect that my student has some sort of medical condition, like autism. Just speaking plainly, many teachers have a lot of knowledge about medical conditions (such as autism, auditory processing problems, ADHD), but we are NOT doctors and should not diagnose anything or even suggest to a parent that we think their child has a medical issue. Period. We can certainly share our concerns with this child's parents, and even create a list of things that we have noted, but we should never indicate that we have suspicions about a diagnosis. If a parent comes to us with concerns and needs assistance, we can certainly direct the parent to the people who will guide in getting help for the child, but we cannot share our speculations about what we think is "wrong" with the child. "Have you discussed this with your pediatrician?" is an appropriate response to these concerns. Sharing our observations (data) for the parent to share with the doctor is appropriate as well. It's also crucial to remember that norms and procedures in school may be very different from what the child has experienced in the past and this may affect the child's behavior/understanding of how to react in certain situations.

This student writes letters and numbers backwards; I think the student may have dyslexia. Is it possible that SLIFE may also have dyslexia? Absolutely. But there are some issues that need to be addressed before we jump to that conclusion.

- Letters and numbers are symbols that we learn to represent concepts. They are meaningless to children until they understand that "symbol-sound/concept" relationship. If children are still in that phase of development and have not yet developed that sense of what these symbols mean and look like, they may very well write them backwards or in an inconsistent manner, especially if their dominant language does not use the same alphabet. This is part of the reason why dyslexia testing is not appropriate for very young children. If our SLIFE are still in that developmental stage, we may find this type of errors in use of these symbols, and it may or may not indicate dyslexia.
- Also, the screening for dyslexia includes activities such as rhyming, which may not be something to which many children have been exposed. Nursery rhymes or songs that many students in the United States hear repeatedly in the pre-school years help them get a sense of that symbol-sound relationship—and that may be something our SLIFE haven't experienced.
- Does the child need a vision screening? Are there issues

associated with occupational therapy, such as fine motor skills or visual-spatial issues? Is there a difference if lines are provided for writing? Do they use an appropriate pencil grip?

- Is the child just completely overwhelmed and exhausted from learning in a different language all day?

There are some inherent issues with those tests that make it challenging to identify if these students have these difficulties, in addition to the effects of their different experiences in education.

Statistically, it is likely that some students who have SLIFE status may also have learning disabilities, only because it is likely that any subset of the population may have learners with disabilities. However, it is important to understand that there are several other factors that influence the academic success of these students. We have to take time to really reflect upon the available resources and services that we provide to these students outside of the special education program to make sure that we meet their unique needs.

Probably the most important thing to remember when working with Newcomers or SLIFE is to teach with dignity and with a growth mindset. It is never, ever appropriate to treat teaching 12-year-olds with materials appropriate for kindergartens. Newcomers' educational level may be at a primary level *temporarily*, but the Newcomers must not be made to feel that they are only capable of what a much younger child can do. Newcomers bring with them life experiences well beyond what 5-year-olds would have, which can help the Newcomers progress much faster with the appropriate supports.

Reflection discussion:

Reflection 1: Literacy in second language instruction is the magic ticket to engagement and language acquisition. No longer do teachers drill lists of unnecessary vocabulary words out of context for students to memorize. If books are used by language teachers, learners can be gaining vocabulary in multimodal fashion while engaging in the four domains of language: listening, speaking, reading and writing. Learners also experience language in action through books, rather than going through lists of words. It is within that context that learners acquire language.

Interacting with words in books can activate other types of problem-solving skills. If students do not recognize a word, the strategies that they can practice not only help with learning vocabulary, they also boost reading proficiency as well. When students read books (or listen as the teacher reads!) and then discuss or write about the story, there are so many skills being honed at the same time.

Engaging learners in books to enhance vocabulary can also help build their schema about the world around them. With younger students, I often use books that have vivid pictures and characters that keep their interest. With older students, I try to include more nonfiction (or even historical fiction) books that will help build their background about the content area while reading and discussing pictures. Graphic novels are also great ways to engage MLs. The thing with books is that there is so much more than words to them.

When I set students up with independent reading books, there are many things to consider that will support their individual successes. First, we have a discussion about what they are looking for in a book. Some students are still only comfortable reading picture books with fewer words and simpler vocabulary. If an older student prefers this, I never say no. Sometimes, it's more about overcoming the feelings of intimidation of reading in the target language than it is the content. Students can certainly write about picture books in terms of describing the pictures or the characters. This is still very valuable literacy time and should not be discounted because of the student's choice of book.

Other times, students may choose books based on the topic rather than the "readability" factor. This is outstanding; students can interact with the book how they see fit. Some students will sit next to the book with a notebook and write down words they feel are important to the story and look up the translations. This can be a long process, but we can definitely support this type of reading if the students are engaged. They are building vocabulary and schema while interacting with a book of their interest. If the book is way beyond the reading level of students, they can interact with the book in unconventional ways. Students can search for unfamiliar vocabulary and draw or write sentences to represent what those words mean. At the end of each chapter, they can write summaries of what they think is happening in the book. They can also write questions about the book and search for the answers ("What is the setting?" "What are the names of the main characters?" "Describe…"). They can choose quotes or paragraphs from the book and write an extension about them as a form of creative writing—which may or may not, in reality, have anything to do with the story. The point is that the ways that students interact with books above their independent reading level *should* be outside the box...and are still very valuable literacy time.

Some people feel that people should read one book at a time in order to fully engage with it. While many people may prefer this, our students do not have to commit to one book at a time. I have seen this compared to television shows; we can be watching more than one program on any given evening, but we only watch one at one particular moment. The other shows do not interfere with our enjoyment of any one, and neither would reading more than one book. If our Newcomers have some literacy in their dominant language, I recommend that students who are reading more than one book can read one in their dominant language and one in the target language. Reading in their dominant language, students can continue to build those skills in a more "natural" way that may come easier to them while reading in the target language can be more exhausting. Alternating between the two may help our Newcomers remember the joy and relaxation of reading in their native language (even if it is at a lower level if that is what their skill set is!) that will build them up for learning to read in English.

Selecting a book by their "just-right" reading level is also a valid way to engage Newcomers into literacy, as hopefully the book will be exactly at the level they need to improve but not too difficult for them. I always think of Vygotsky's (1978) Zone of Proximal Development as a tennis match. In this situation, we don't want our students to play against someone whose skill set is so below their own that they will not have to practice any of their best shots. And we don't want them playing against someone so much better that they give up. Playing against someone just a little bit better than they are will keep them sharpening their skills in order to keep in the game. The last match-up is the "just right" book. And as long as the book is chosen jointly for reading level and for interest, this is an effective way to engage in reading.

As a final note about independent reading books, I often encourage historical fiction books if the students find that this is an interest for them. Not only are they getting experience reading fiction with characters, setting and the like, but they are building schema about times and events in history that maybe they didn't have beforehand. However, if this isn't their "jam," then find out what is!

Reflection 2: The issue of whether or not Newcomers or SLIFE should be evaluated for special education services is an extremely controversial one. There really cannot be one specific answer that fits all students, but there can—and should—be a lot of discussion about the individual, unique needs of each child. Sometimes those needs can be met through intense intervention with an ESL specialist and support from the classroom teacher and sometimes this child needs the help of a special education teacher.

Special education services must only be reserved for students who have a documented learning disability or a medical problem for which they require an Individualized Education Plan (IEP) to provide them access to the curriculum. To be clear, this is different from a student who has missed time in school or who has language differences. Just because a student may have missed concepts or skills due to missed (or different?) schooling, this does not mean that the student has a learning disability. The student may be an excellent learner, but **lacked opportunity and experience**—this is not a reason to classify a student as needing special education services. This child may very well need intervention to help bridge the educational gaps and additional support to access curricula, but may not necessarily need an IEP. Sometimes time and intervention are all that a student may need to find success in learning; a teacher's patience and knowledge about meeting the needs of SLIFE can be all the student needs.

Additionally, just because students speak another language does not mean that they are "low" learners or that they are at a disadvantage when it comes to learning. Although it may take some time for them to learn content in a different language, they may be average—or even gifted—learners. Some educators feel that if a student has not mastered English in some sort of predetermined timetable, the student should be considered for an IEP. Learning a language is not always an easy task, even for people who have an aptitude for language learning, and a student's progress/success in language acquisition is based upon many variables. A language difference does not equal special education services. Period.

With this being said, it does not mean that Newcomers or SLIFE should never be determined as eligible for special education services. Just because a student comes from another country speaking another language does not mean that the student cannot have a learning disability or a medical reason for an IEP. As with any subset of the population, there will be some students who have special education needs; their other circumstances do not negate this fact.

Some districts have specific amounts of time that students must be in the country before being evaluated for special education—and there are good reasons behind this—but there should not be a "one-size-fits-all" rule prohibiting these evaluations. While I absolutely appreciate giving time to Newcomers to ensure that they will not be classified erroneously, there are some cases in which it is a disservice to the child if we do not address needs through an IEP. Following are some suggestions for things to investigate before bringing students up to be considered for evaluations for special education services:

- What does the parent say on the Home Language Survey? Does the parent report that there were previous difficulties in school? Is there reported to be an underlying medical condition or concern for this child?
- Does the child communicate or understand well in the dominant language? If teachers or staff can speak this language, does the child have the ability to follow simple directions?
- Does the child have knowledge of literacy or mathematics appropriate to the amount and type of schooling the child has had?
- As time goes by and the child acclimates more to school, does the child demonstrate progress with literacy or math? If the child receives intervention or additional support, has data shown improvement? Has the child shown an increased understanding of school norms and procedures?
- Teachers must take care never to "diagnose" any child (we may be experts, but we are not doctors!), but if there is behavior that is extremely out of the ordinary or alarming, be sure to contact the child's parents for a conference right away. If appropriate in your district, ask a member of the

Child Study Team (school psychologist, social worker, learning specialists) to give some feedback about what they see as well. Teachers can certainly document their concerns and provide that data for parents to share with their child's pediatrician to help give a well-rounded view of what may be going on with their child.

- When meeting with parents, do they report medical or educational issues in the past? Sometimes parents may share this information when educators are sharing their current concerns. ***"In our country, doctors were very worried about her and thought she had mental retardation. That's why we came here to get help for her"***—translated. While this information does not indicate that there is certainly this type of diagnosis, it can give us a perspective on the challenges of this student.

These suggestions are not meant to determine for sure if a student should be evaluated for special education services. As stated previously, these decisions are as individual as the student and should be treated as such. Overall, teachers should not rush to refer students to the Child Study Team, but there should not be hard or inflexible guidelines preventing teachers from reaching out if it's clear that a child should at least be considered for evaluations. While there may be challenges (even for professionals!) in determining when difficulties are part of language acquisition or when they are results of learning disabilities, all should be on board with doing whatever possible will help a child who is struggling.

For lists for reading engagement tips to share with parents (in English and Spanish) and suggestions for ways to scaffold for MLs, please look in the appendix.

8

ASSESSMENT

> *"We must keep in mind the purposes of our assessment. Is it to punish the student who did not understand? Or is it to determine what needs to be revisited in instruction? How far has the student come and in which direction should the instruction take them?"*

Reflection questions:

- As a non-tenured teacher, how do/did you feel when you have an unannounced observation? Did it feel different from an announced observation? Did you ever receive feedback that you felt was unreasonable?
- What was the feeling in your house while you were growing up on report card day?

Different types of assessments

Assessments are certainly not one-size-fits-all, nor should they be. There are different purposes for assessments and they should be approached in appropriate fashions.

Formative assessment includes ways to assess learning that determine what the student has either mastered or still needs to learn. This should then determine next steps in terms of instruction, intervention, remediation, or enrichment. This most certainly is crucial when working with MLs, Newcomers, and SLIFE. Results of formative assessments help teachers determine what types of scaffolds that students need—as it is important not to give more support or assistance than necessary for students to progress. These types of assessments may be formal (tests, projects, quizzes) or informal (anecdotal notes, exit tickets, self evaluations, classwork). Students are often part of the formative assessment process and see the results of how instruction is designed based on the results. Formative assessment is a means of communication between students and teachers.

Summative assessments are those end-of-unit tests that determine mastery of a concept or topic before moving on to the next. I view these as a double-edged sword. The students who do well on these assessments feel validated, but the students who do not do well feel defeated. And the purpose of these tests are not necessarily to go back to reteach these concepts, as are formative assessments. These defeated students move on to the next concept and hope that they have a better understanding of the coming unit. I'm certainly not saying that summative assessments are not necessary, but it's difficult to support if teachers consider this as the way to put a bow on a unit and move on. These types of assessments may wind up being punitive in nature (whether or not that is the initial intent) when grades bring negative consequences.

There are standardized assessments for MLs which are tests that are given across a large area, whether by state or national standards. These can be considered "high-stakes" tests because they can affect placement for students and evaluations for staff or districts. Some of the standardized assessments for the entire population of students have different "rules" for MLs, especially Newcomers. Some states exempt Newcomers for the first year in English Language Arts and will allow them to take the Mathematics portion in the student's native language if available. This is reasonable for students who have been educated in their native language and whose schools teach math vocabulary/concepts similarly to the way it is tested in the student's new country. However, some Newcomers or SLIFE are tested on things that they have not had the opportunity to learn. The second year, Newcomers may be required to take the grade-level English Language Arts assessment in English that often represents a challenge for native speakers. MLs are usually entitled to extended time and small groups while testing, and sometimes they are able to get the questions read aloud to them. I do understand the importance of standardized testing to track progress for students from year-to-year and to give more information about targeted instruction that students may need. I just have a hard time putting students through experiences like this.

Multilingual learners also have their own specific brand of standardized testing that is designed to determine their status as eligible for ESL services. In many states, this test is ACCESS for ELLs or other WIDA assessments. Our students take an English language proficiency test each winter or spring to both see progress and to see if they demonstrate the language proficiency needed to exit ESL services. The four domains of language are tested and the reports are reflective of how students score in each of the domains. In the spring of 2020, as we entered virtual learning, some of our students did not take our annual ESL standardized assessment. As much as I dislike this type of testing (just being honest!), I found that we were at a loss of valuable data and information about proficiency and progress in the domains of language. There definitely is value in these types of assessments, as long as they are only one "piece of the puzzle" and students' strengths and progress are assessed in an authentic way.

Other standardized assessments that MLs may be required to complete include district-level benchmark assessments, which should mirror the accessibility features and modifications of state-level testing. To be clear, translating the English version of these assessments into the dominant language of your students is NOT sufficient in terms of making these tests accessible. There are other aspects to these assessments that must be considered before determining if they are culturally appropriate for diverse learners, such as linguistic questions that are specific to English or cultural bias.

There are also times in which students are referred to the Child Study Team for evaluations to determine if they have needs that would be best served by an IEP (Individualized Education Plan). While this should certainly not be the "norm" for MLs (language difference is NOT a disability!), there may be times in which MLs have needs that go beyond missed education or language difference.

Assessing Newcomers and SLIFE in the classroom

Assessments can be very effective for helping teachers meet the needs of our Newcomers and SLIFE as long as they are done intentionally and the results guide instruction or intervention. The most important thing that teachers must do, however, is to ensure that the atmosphere in the classroom is not anxiety-producing for these students when they are being assessed. Teachers must establish that formative tasks demonstrate what students have already mastered and still need to reinforce—and that they are equally accepted. If done regularly and with a positive perspective, these tasks and assessments are essential to true evaluation. As with all students, we focus on engagement and "showing what you know," rather than catching them in what they don't know.

Assessments may be modified for MLs to allow them to demonstrate understanding of the material and language of the content area. These can be modified in several different ways, depending upon the design of the assessment. Remember that different students (and different MLs) may require different modifications. We do not always expect our newer students to be at the point at which they get every single concept you are teaching. They are learning language and content at the same time—if they get the basics/important points of content along with the language, we are finding success.

Teachers may:

- Reduce the number of words in the questions to make them as clear as possible.
- Highlight (or bold/underline/italicize) key words in instructions to help students differentiate important directions.
- Provide a word bank when possible or appropriate to the task.
- Allow students to use a dictionary or translation technology when producing or interpreting language if needed.
- Offer multiple choice: Simplify language. Reduce the number of answer choices. Highlight (or type in bold) vocabulary that was a focus in class.
- Provide matching activities: Choose really crucial language/vocabulary. Either students can match to the definition in English or write a translation in Spanish if appropriate.
- Allow labeling: Visuals are a great way to include MLs. They can label, or even if you provide a visual, they can explain what it is or the importance of it.

- Permit drawing or sketchnoting to demonstrate understanding of many concepts.
- Allow students to write in as much the target language as possible, but use their native language as needed (depending upon language proficiency level).
- Create a different rubric to assess content and language appropriate for students' language proficiency level.

Students understand language much before they are able to produce it. So, sometimes a check for understanding may be a "thumbs up" or a visual signal instead of a verbal response. Multiple-choice questions or matching may also be a good start for assessing understanding (although the ultimate goal is to assess using productive language and higher-level thinking skills!). Drawing or sketching may also be a basic way that MLs can demonstrate understanding.

Students can write summaries, and the way they write can be differentiated. Some students will write mainly in their dominant language and that is perfectly acceptable. When they finish, they can determine important words that they can look up and translate into English. Some could be the vocabulary that was highlighted previously in class if appropriate to the answer. As students become more confident in writing in English, you can expect more English in their written responses.

Different ways of showing understanding without producing language are great ways of assessing understanding, too. If drawing, categorizing, or even creating Google docs with pictures found on the internet could work for your particular skill/concept, that may be an opportunity to show understanding in a nonconventional way.

Collaborative learning groups are key to supporting Newcomers and MLs in learning content and language, but many wonder about how they would evaluate their learning. Teachers should consider how they assess other students—and modify if necessary! For instance, beginning with grouping MLs with other students who possibly speak the dominant language of the Newcomers (or who are very patient and friendly!) to help them acclimate to this "new" type of learning is effective. While in groups, teachers should consider having the ML work in a role where they are able to utilize their assets to contribute (drawing, looking up information). There are ways to empower our students and assess their strengths while they are forging relationships with their peers.

Grades and report cards

There has been a lot of discourse lately about grades and whether or not the importance of grades as a valid form of feedback is equitable for students across the board. People who are in favor of maintaining the current grading system may argue:

- Grades are ways that students can get feedback on their work and learning.
- Grades are motivation for students to work hard.
- Grades are extrinsic rewards.
- Grades give indications of whether a student has mastered the curricula.
- Grades are means of communication between school and home.
- Grades can give outside sources (colleges?) information about the students.
- Grades can help determine placement in different classes or programs.

Others may feel that the current grading system may have some inherent bias within the evaluations.

- Some students may simply have a better chance of "gathering points" than others.

- Assignments are often graded as they are completed, rather than whether the content was mastered.
- Late assignments may receive lower grades, but this does not indicate understanding.
- Some teachers grade for content, others for presentation or grammar.
- Perceptions of student effort are often part of the grade.
- Grading policies may be inconsistent among teachers.
- Behavior is sometimes a factor in grades.
- Sometimes grades are far more subjective than objective.
- Grades may have punitive aspects (failure, ineligibility for sports, summer school).

With both perspectives in mind, where does that put our Newcomers or SLIFE students in terms of grading? It is good practice to take the grading out of the equation for these students for a period of time after they first arrive (two marking periods is a common suggestion or depending upon the proficiency level as determined by standardized tests) with "No grade" or a pass/fail option. This helps the teacher and the student focus on progress and less on numbers. This also gives the teacher time to *formatively* evaluate where the student is in terms of prior learning and skills. Gill writes a narrative for each of her Newcomers to go home with the report card that explains what they have been learning and how they are progressing and offers suggestions for how their families can support the child's growth at home. Armed with this information, the teacher, the student, and the family can then embark on the journey of education-—together.

When Newcomers have been in the district for a number of months and it is "time" for grades to come into play, there are many different ways to accomplish this. As we have stated, it is important to assess understanding and that these students have access to grade-appropriate curricula. However, it is clear that many Newcomers or SLIFE may not have the language ability or the educational background to find success equal to their native-speaking peers (nor should one expect them to!). So, if these students are now earning grades for the report cards on grade-level standards, there must be supports, scaffolds, and modifications for some. These grades should reflect their achievement on grade-level work with the supports in place. In order to indicate this on the report card (which is often "compared" to peers or to district norms—whether or not that may be best practice!), a simple indication that the student is an ML is all that is necessary. This indicates that these students may not have the same individual mastery as perhaps a student who does not need the scaffolds, but this is an evaluation of a student who is learning the target language.

It is important to note that they should not be "failing" if they are engaged and progressing in content and language (there goes that subjectivity again in grades!). And if students are not completing assignments and "earn" 0s as grades, how is progress being noted for these students? If Newcomers and SLIFE are engaged in learning—and failing—teachers (and the district) must reflect on what they can do differently to meet the needs of these children. Period.

Melissa and her colleagues write individual narratives for MLs in their middle-school science classes. This allows them to specifically identify the strengths and areas to improve for these students without assigning a "number" to their growth and progress. These narratives are included in the students' files along with their report cards and include information on content and language mastery.

Reflection discussion:

Reflection 1: Observation days are stressful, even for the most seasoned veteran teacher. Sometimes we are comfortable with the person who is evaluating us, and other times we've heard horror stories about the observations that an administrator wrote. There are many variables that contribute to a "successful" or a "challenging" evaluation and some of them may be out of the control of the teacher.

Many people prefer the unannounced observation because they already feel confident in what they do every day and indicate that they don't want to feel like they have to "put on a show" for an observer. Others who like these types of observations may become so nervous at the prospect of being observed that they would prefer not to know when someone is coming. These unannounced visits flow with what the teacher had already planned for a regular day.

Teachers who are more comfortable with announced observations may just not enjoy that moment in which the principal enters the room with a laptop ready to observe. They may be just as prepared and confident on a daily basis but prefer to be aware about any changes of routine that may occur.

The issue is that everyone has their own preferences and comfort zones about how they are evaluated. If an observation is more like a *formative assessment* of the teacher in which the principal is part of the team to help the teacher reflect and grow, the observation may be a more positive experience. If the observation turns out to be a punitive experience in which the end result is not concerned with helping the teacher improve, one may feel like our Newcomers are feeling if they see failing grades on their report cards without an idea of how they can do better.

Reflection 2: Report card day in some houses is like a birthday—students run home to their parents, waving the good news and waiting to celebrate. Other students may dread the day worse than getting their vaccinations. Feelings can run the spectrum on these days, yet for many teachers, it's just another day at the office.

We teachers sometimes forget the feelings that students may associate with those grades and those comments. Some students feel like the grades they receive are personal reflections on how the teachers feel about them as a person. If they do well, the teacher must like them and is surely proud of them. If they do poorly, the teacher hates them and thinks they can't learn.

As teachers, we must create an environment in which grades are important...but progress, effort, improvement, and self-esteem are more important. I have had many conversations with students in which I told them that grades do not define them. Grades are a piece to the puzzle of their educational experience, not the whole thing.

If grades are to be considered to be part of the home-school communication, then follow-up and explanation are absolutely necessary. Sometimes, there is little consistency among grades, classes, and schools in terms of grading and criteria. In my own children's school, they changed to standards-based grading a few years ago for grades K-4. As an educator, I see the value in those types of grades and really understand that teachers can then communicate how well the students have mastered particular concepts within a subject area. As a parent...if I'm being honest, those grades are less concrete and meaningful for us. If I feel that way, I imagine that various grading systems may be less than clear for our students' families.

Assessments and the corresponding evaluations and data must be viewed in ways that are useful for students, teachers, and families. Grading must be less about keeping kids accountable and more about authentic feedback and growth—for both the educators and the students.

Please find a sample Newcomer curriculum pacing guide in the appendix.

9

PARENT/FAMILY PERSPECTIVE

Your students' parents are sending the "best kids they have." Have patience with the kids and have empathy for their parents.

Reflection questions:

- What types of ways were your own parents involved in your schooling? If you are a parent, what are your experiences with your child's school? How have your educational experiences with your family affected your interactions with your students' parents?
- What effects does parental involvement have within the school community? What can teachers do to involve parents who may not appear to engage in their child's education for a variety of reasons? What school/community events are you drawn to as an adult? Which do you feel are "chores" or an annoyance?

Hoping for success

As an undergraduate student at The College of New Jersey in my first education class, my professor said something to me that I'll never forget: "These parents aren't keeping their 'better' kids at home. They are sending **their very best kids** to you in your classroom. So view those children as such, even the really challenging ones." In other words, instead of getting resentful or judgmental of parents, just know that we all want what's best for the children. Parents are not sending their children to school and hoping that they do not find success. As an enthusiastic future teacher, I didn't quite understand what he meant, but as the years went on (and I became a parent!), it really resonated with me.

Our students' parents' perspectives are not something that typically is covered in district professional development or in pre-service preparation for teaching any student, let alone MLs. But no matter what the situation is, families of Newcomers have gone through some major transitions or possibly trauma in their journeys, so it's something that is crucial for teachers to understand. In addition to helping our Newcomers reach their potential at school, it's up to the school community to ensure that the family is able to support them as well.

Supporting our new students and their parents begins the minute they walk through the doors to register. The welcoming environment, the assistance of navigating the unknown world of school, and the information needed in order to prepare for school all provide the support for the entire family that is so necessary. I often try to speak to a Newcomer's parents on the first day just to soothe nerves and let them know that their child is safe and doing well. We can only imagine what the parents are feeling as they send their children off to a place in which they do not speak the language or understand the norms. I recall how I felt sending my own children to kindergarten (or even high school!) and my kids do speak the language spoken in the school.

Separated families

The decision to move to another country is never one made lightly. Sometimes the entire family moves, but other times there are family members who are left behind for long periods of time or indefinitely. ***"I left my son in Guatemala eleven years ago and he just came up to me five months ago. Sometimes I still look at him and see the little baby that I used to know"***—translated. Sometimes a parent will go ahead to the new country to establish himself or herself before sending for other family members. When their child may finally arrive, parent and child may essentially be strangers. This is obviously a struggle for many families and certainly may contribute to the stress and trauma our students experience.

Many students report also leaving siblings and other close relatives behind when moving to the new country. ***"I am here now with only my brother, who is 23. My parents are back in my old country"***—translated. It is essential that we understand the layers of support that families in this situation may need. Screenings with our school nurses Sue and Marta helped us realize that this Newcomer has limited vision and difficulty hearing; living with only his brother in a new country made it difficult for him to get exams or services that he needs. Also, feelings of homesickness, uncertainty, guilt, and loss may be experienced, especially when children leave caretakers or siblings close in age. Sometimes, the family left behind plans on coming to the new country at some point, and other times our students may fear never seeing them again. The uncertainty and grief of a separated family unit add another layer of adjustment for our students.

O was my first Newcomer as a young teacher. He arrived in April of his 6th-grade year and had a smile that would light up the classroom. He quickly made friends in our class and his teachers forged a special connection with him. O had traveled to the United States with his sister as UMs (Unaccompanied Minors) to live with his father whom they hadn't seen in eight years. His brother and beloved mother stayed behind. We had a conference with his father about how hard O worked and how much he was progressing at the beginning of June and his father was bursting with pride. O loved school and came every day with a great attitude. His father told us how much O missed his mother, but they were hoping to one day bring her and his brother to the United States.

I remember giving O a hug on the last day of school and telling him we would see him in September. Two days later, one day before his 13th birthday, he committed suicide.

We'll never know why O did this, but we knew how much he missed his mother and we have always suspected that it just may have been too much for him. The memory of O is a constant reminder for me that we must really work to meet the needs of ALL our students, but especially those who have been through loss and trauma. Part of me thinks that the prospect of not having school for the next months—and maybe school being a release or safe haven—contributed to his actions. We may not know the troubles that our students may be carrying or the horrors they have experienced, but we can support them and let them know that we welcome them with joy in our class—and our hearts. I know we at least did that for O, even if we may have missed some other sign that he needed help.

Separated families can be a challenging burden for our Newcomers, like our O. With this being said, teachers have the responsibility to do their best to support these students—but must remember not to shoulder it themselves. Some of the grief or challenges with which our students and their families are dealing need the expertise of a team, rather than a teacher taking everything alone. Guidance counselors, community liaisons, school psychologists, or appropriate personnel should be involved. Often, towns have services for immigrants with multilingual specialists who can help these families access services available within the community.

I have recently heard judgment being placed on parents who choose to move to another country with their children and enter without documentation, who separate their families, or who send their children as Unaccompanied Minors to another country. *How could someone do that to their children? They are at fault for putting their children in danger. They must be horrible parents to do something like this. I would never!* I cannot be more clear: No one knows the situations in which these families lived prior to making these (or any) decisions and NO ONE has any right to pass judgment. We all have our sense of what is "right" or "wrong" in our lives, but until we have walked in someone's shoes who has had to make these choices, there is no room for our opinions.

Shining the spotlight?

Newcomers' families come to our country under many different circumstances and from many different countries. Documentation is an issue for some, but not others. As educators, we must be sure not to assume status, and we must also never use the word "illegal." *No human being is illegal.* I often liken this to a child being called a "bad kid." We may not agree with this child's behavior or choices, but that does not indicate that this label should be given to the human being rather than the actions. Our students' families' experiences have many layers to them, only a few of which we may understand.

Many families of our MLs live in fear in their new country, whether they are documented or undocumented. This may include many different types of fears: fear of the unknown, physical safety, making the right choices for their family, financial worries, and many more. Some parents say that they do not even come to the school because they do not want to put a target on their backs for legal attention. They might not report when a crime is being committed against them because they prefer to stay out of the radar. Landlords may sometimes not be in accordance with heat or water because they know their tenants will not file a formal report against them. They may also get taken advantage of in terms of work without legal recourse.

While it's very difficult to determine what "shines a spotlight" on a person without documentation, the school should be a welcoming and safe environment for all students and their families. We as educators have a variety of political and social beliefs and background experiences (one of the beautiful things about our profession!), but we have the amazing responsibility to teach every student who enters our classroom, no matter what that family's legal status is. Our students must feel safe with us, as should their families. Schools can be a resource for educational support in the evenings, whether they offer parenting classes, PTA meetings, or English lessons; the more that these families are present in the schools, the more welcome they'll feel. For many of our students' families, school is the first connection they can make to become engaged in their new country. That's a big responsibility for educators.

The hopes for their family's future

As students learn English in school, there may be an unfortunate focus on what they feel they "lack" in language, but in their "outside life," they may be turnkeying this information for the benefit of their family. ***"I need help in English so I can get a good grade and learn more. I teach to my brother and my parents in talk English at my house."*** They feel as if they do not know much at school, but are often becoming the experts at home. Even young children may translate for their parents at doctor's offices, school meetings, and other types of appointments. Sarah recalls a middle-school student coming to her after school to learn how to balance a checkbook and write checks; as he was "good at math," this was his job in the household. Although this is extremely helpful for their families, we must also recognize the amount of pressure that some of these children may feel under these responsibilities. Again, we do not judge; we support and build up these families.

Many teachers find that these families will support their children in school in any way that they can. ***"You must "echar ganas" in school in order to be successful in life"***—translated. This phrase "*echar ganas*" is so much more than the translation: *to have the drive or motivation to succeed* is a rough translation. But in many Hispanic cultures, it represents their lives in their new country. They've put their lives on the line for their children; those kids now have the responsibility to put everything they have into working towards success. Their parents have sacrificed so much to provide their children this opportunity to learn and work hard. These sacrifices are an investment in their children's futures.

Reflection questions:

Reflection 1: Thinking about how my own parents were involved in our schooling really helps put the position of our students' families in perspective for me. As a teacher, I go into meetings for my own children with confidence that I know the law and I know my rights as a parent and my child's rights as a student. This has been extremely helpful to me, as I have been in meetings in which I would have been intimidated if I did not have expertise in this area. My parents were not in education and did not know the ins and outs of school, but were supportive from afar. My mother went to conferences and was supportive of my schooling, but it was not necessarily her wheelhouse. I could imagine how my mother would have had even more difficulty in supporting my education if she also did not have a strong command of the language being spoken by the teachers.

As a parent, I have never had to fight for my child's rights in a language that is not native to me. However, I have been in the situation in which I have had to advocate for my child who has challenges. The battles I have had to fight for my kids are very different from those my mother had, but they all have those same feelings behind them: a combination of fear, fury, and desperation to get your child what the child needs. I've sat at those tables with tears in my eyes and my heart in my throat. And I know with certainty that the parents of our students feel those same emotions as well.

I have been on the teacher's side of the conference table for many of my MLs, as well. Our students' parents may not speak the language, nor have a working knowledge of the intricacies of Child Study Team meetings, intervention services, IEPs, or 504s. While in those meetings, teachers must put themselves in the place of those parents, probably coming into the school with their hearts on their sleeves. (As I write this, I tear up and those feelings are a pit in my stomach.) These parents need someone to advise them of ways to support their children and what their rights are at these meetings. Educators must consider that—even if the meeting is translated in the dominant language of the family—educational vocabulary is very specific and not always easily understood. Also, it may be part of some families' cultures not to question the teacher; this is the teacher's domain and the teacher knows best for the children. Providing an environment in which parents are an integral part of the "discussion," rather than simply on the receiving end of information, is crucial. ALL families of our students need to know that the school is on their side (*which is the side of the child,* ***always***).

<u>Reflection 2:</u> Parental involvement in schools has a huge impact on our students. When students understand that their parents and teachers are a united front in support of the children, it means the world for the children's confidence and motivation. The students feel that their success is important to a group of people, and they may have more feelings of positivity about their triumphs.

Additionally, parents who feel welcome and are able to attend functions at the school have background about school to have conversations with their children about how the school day went. They can put a face to the name when discussing the teachers and administrators and can also picture the classroom, the gym, hallways, or cafeteria. They are also in contact with the teachers, which can improve academic communication between family and school and also forge a bond to support academics in the house. This will increase the parents' understanding of what is being taught in school and help "keep them in the game."

Very often teachers are looking for parental involvement when the child is struggling, whether it is academically or behaviorally. And we have all heard the judgmental comments from teachers about parents never showing up for their children. It is crucial that positive communication is the norm for these parents (really, for all parents, but parents of Newcomers, especially). If parents often get positive communication from teachers, they will be more supportive when their children need that home-school connection to help them succeed.

Although there are a variety of reasons that parents may have as to why they do not regularly participate in activities in their children's schools, teachers can reach out in many ways in a positive fashion to help build connections.

- Send home positive notes in the language that the parents speak. Use Google translate if necessary—we are focusing on communication over grammar and correctness. Not only does this positively engage parents, but this also shows a value for the home language of the family and a willingness to include that language in the teacher's linguistic repertoire.
- Newsletters in the students' languages are helpful as well and can include pictures and give parents an idea of what is going on in the classroom. These communications can showcase some information and culture from the homes of the students in the class. Not everything must be in all

languages, but representation matters. Again, Google translate can be a useful tool, as well as the visuals.

- However, some parents do not read well, even in their native language. Then you can print a picture of their child working diligently (or laughing, or any sort of positive picture) with emojis that can express how well the child is doing. At that point, the words do not matter; it's the fact that you are reaching out to the parent in a positive way that counts.
- If your students' parents tend to have cell phones or access to the internet, apps like Seesaw or Remind can help parents stay in the loop with what's going on in class. Pictures can be shared with specific parents, as well.
- Positive calls home are great if you or a colleague can communicate in the language of the parents. Keeping a current phone number on file is important—yet challenging—for new students as cell phone numbers may change often. To be clear, the only requirement for communication is to be understood; you do not have to speak perfectly (or even correctly) for the message to be received.
- A multilingual section of the district website can provide parents access to the morning announcements of the schools. A Twitter account can also be used for this purpose.
- A multilingual "welcome packet" can give parents information about the school and introduce key players in their child's education. Calendars and emergency procedures/drills may be explained here, as well as important events, such as conferences or open houses. Some districts offer this electronically and provide some videos of what emergency drills look like; the effectiveness of this depends upon whether or not the parents typically have access to the internet.
- Offering a variety of times to be available to meet or speak

with parents can help make their child's education accessible to them, other than the standard 6 p.m. conference time.

Parents are hoping for the very, very best as they send their children to school, especially in a new country. Some may feel as if their heart is on their sleeve, especially those first days and weeks. Educators may sometimes have prior conceptions about the types of behaviors they feel parents should exhibit in order to be "supportive." A fresh perspective is necessary to see the whole picture—for the benefit of the child.

10

REMOTE LEARNING CHALLENGES

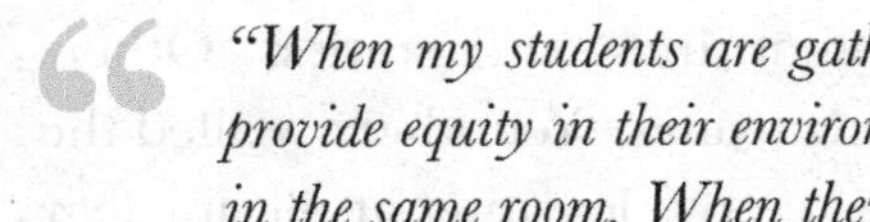

"When my students are gathered in my classroom, I can at least provide equity in their environment at that time; they are all seated in the same room. When they are learning from home, there are so many inequities that I just can't fix for them."

Reflection questions:

- How do you feel when you have unexpected visitors at your home?
- Are there things in your own life that you would prefer not to share with your class or with your department? How would it affect your willingness to participate if you were forced to open up about them in public?

"At first I was excited for school at home. But now I think how hard it is for me to learn like this. Everything is so complicated. I hope we go back to regular school soon"

— TRANSLATED

What does remote instruction look like?

When we first began remote instruction in March of 2020, this was uncharted territory for all of us. With literally no advanced notice, we had to dive head first into figuring out what this was going to look like and how we were going to best meet the diverse needs of our students. Some districts created packets of learning for different content areas and grades. Others relied on technology to help facilitate learning. Yet others "called the whole thing off" and did not pursue remote learning at all, for fear of leaving some students out. There are also districts who pursued a combination of more than one of these methods. While obviously there are underlying reasons for districts to choose different protocols to follow for remote learning, each has its own challenges.

While experiencing the pandemic of 2020, some school districts decided to simply **cancel school** rather than trying to reach their students in different ways. When explaining why they chose to do this, there are several different types of responses. Some felt that there was no way that they could meet the needs of students as directed by their IEPs (Individualized Education Plans) and feared that they would face legal trouble if they continued with school without specifically addressing their accommodations. Others thought that school closure would be a short-term event and it wasn't worth the time that it would take to get together the work for the students. These school districts may also not want any danger from giving anyone—even staff—access to the schools during a closure that is because of a virus. The issue of not being able to provide equitable access to work is also a reason why some districts declined to participate in remote instruction.

There are obvious challenges to closing the schools and canceling class for all students. There is significant loss of instruction during this time, which will affect students both presently and in the upcoming academic years. Curricula will have to be readdressed, as students have not covered what was previously planned. Most importantly, however, are the other needs that are addressed while school is in session that will be missed if it is completely closed. Many students rely on school lunches or packaged food that comes from the school to keep hunger at bay. Some students live in less-than-ideal situations and their experiences and relationships in school help keep them safe from abuse or neglect. Socio-emotional needs are also extremely important and something that may fall by the wayside with no contact with school staff or classmates.

Districts who distribute **paper copies of assignments** may do so to promote a "level playing field" for all students, regardless of socio-economic status. Staff determines worksheets, workbooks, or text-books that will be available for students to use at home to continue their studies during remote instruction. These packets should not be introducing new material; rather, they are meant to support students as they are reviewing and reinforcing concepts that they have already learned with their teachers during face-to-face instruction. Students can access this with or without internet access or technology and the work is something that students do not have to figure out how to teach themselves (or depend on family members to teach them).

The logistics of collecting materials and creating packets are very complicated and time consuming. These packets must be made available to all students, so there must either be a system for delivery or pickup. This work cannot necessarily be monitored as to who is completing it and there is certainly a "shelf life" for how many days/weeks students will have engaging tasks before the collection of work must begin again. Also, clearly if students are receiving packets with the purpose of only reviewing and reinforcing, new content is not being learned. Unless specific differentiation is done at the time of the creation of the packets, this type of schooling is "one size fits all" in a situation in which there are many diverse needs. Curricula of upcoming grades must also be considered as students are not moving forward with learning through these packets.

Virtual learning, or learning through the means of technology, is a way of instruction that may include real-time interaction or access to digital tools to facilitate learning. Through different platforms such as Google Classroom, Schoology, or Canvas, teachers can provide students with a variety of synchronous or asynchronous formats of instruction. Links to videos with subtitles in various languages can help build schema for students who do not have the previous years of spiraling instruction in content areas. Teachers can screencast lessons so MLs can watch lessons many times in order to internalize the content or understand the vocabulary. Formative assessments are instantaneous and instruction can be adjusted as needed.

Some districts provide their students with a combination of more than one of these types of instruction. This may depend upon the age of the students, the content area, or the particular needs of different populations. Whatever combination that is sustained during school closures, it certainly must not be determined by lack of accessibility to technology or instructional materials.

This is simply not equitable.

Considerations for virtual, hybrid, and concurrent instruction

It is generally understood that virtual instruction may be the most effective way to teach during a school closure, but there are several variables which must be addressed in order for all students to have access to the educational experiences. All students having access to the internet and technological devices is critical to implementation of this model...but that is just the first step to success. If districts (and families!) are 1:1 with devices and have worked out hotspots for families in need of them, this is the first major hurdle that is overcome.

While working in the face-to-model of instruction, some classes work consistently within digital platforms throughout the school year. These students may have transitioned to virtual learning much easier than others who had to quickly adapt to new platforms that were not already established as part of the classroom norm. Navigating these various platforms (as teachers themselves may be learning them!) is a challenge, particularly for students who may have few skills in technology prior to arriving in their new school. Add to this caregivers who may not be technologically savvy and there may be a whole lot of frustration going on in this home.

The dilemma between synchronous (keeping a consistent class time with the teacher) and asynchronous (structured assignments, flexible timing, teacher availability) instruction is a testy one when discussing virtual instruction. Much like many things, the optimal design would not be either one in isolation; a healthy combination is engaging and builds on the strengths of the students.

Synchronous instruction often includes some type of *video chat*, but this can also include *real-time commentary* on student work, teachers being *available for questions* while the students are working, *interactive games*, or the use of *chat features* in which students and teachers can interact. These interactions can rebuild community and relationships among learners who are lonely and struggling on their own.

If teachers utilize synchronous instructions, they must be aware that flexibility is key. I have seen teachers "giving credit" (or taking points off!) for students speaking or showing their face during video chats. As much as we may like to require face-to-face contact, there are many variables that affect a child's participation, much of which are connected with equity.

Asynchronous instruction may include *screencasts* (videos of the screen with the teacher's voice explaining the lesson or concepts), presentations with *links* or *reading passages*, or pre-assigned tasks with materials that students have with them. Students may be working on these assignments at any time and not necessarily at the same time as the teacher is available. Teachers may have "office hours" or times in which they are available for support or direct instruction, but students complete work at their pace in their time.

While interpersonal communication is crucial during times of school closure, we shouldn't discount the value of having recordings to which our students can listen as many times as necessary in order to understand and learn the vocabulary. Working at one's own pace is sometimes necessary when learning content in two languages. With that being said, interaction is the key to improving proficiency and confidence in the target language. As we know very well, our goals for content and language acquisition for our MLs are equally as important.

As districts consider the health needs of their communities, we have seen a shift to include other methods of education. In addition to purely virtual instruction or full-time in-person instruction, there are other combinations of the two modalities. **Hybrid models** include varying percentages of in-person instruction available (usually 3-5 days a week, with an option for a shortened day), while students still have the option to learn virtually. These students who are learning virtually may be in a different class of students who are all virtual, or they may be joining in the in-person sessions of their peers. Those classrooms with students both at home and in person are using a **concurrent teaching model**.

There are obvious considerations within these different models for Newcomers. We can all acknowledge that in-person instruction has many academic benefits for these students, but here are some other positives:

- They have opportunities to interact with their peers—even in a socially distant environment.
- They can meet adults in person (teachers, admin, counselors) who may be resources for them now or in the future.
- They navigate the school and community every day, with opportunities to hear and speak with others (in many languages). Even the trip between school and home is full of learning opportunities.
- Those who are still learning technology will have more concrete support.
- In-person learning may help Newcomers feel less isolated and give more opportunities to connect with their peers and teachers.

This is not to say that there are no benefits to learning virtually for MLs. Instant breakout rooms allowed me to work in small groups quickly and efficiently—and move among groups or from class-to-class in seconds. Within small groups, students may feel more comfortable asking questions or speaking out loud, especially if the teacher does not always require cameras. As we want to ensure that our MLs spend as much time as possible with their native-English-speaking peers, quick breakout rooms to clarify concepts allow students to leave only for short times to return to the group quickly. Additionally, while with the whole group, the chat and other visual features are very effective in supporting vocabulary development or leveraging dominant languages to build schema.

Equity in remote instruction

As mentioned before, **equity** is not the same for everyone. It's not equitable to assume that all students need the same scaffolds, assignments, or modifications to achieve the same goals. However, part of equity is that all students are given the supports they need to access the grade-level content of their peers. In remote instruction, there is an additional layer of access that must be provided—and that is the responsibility of the school to provide it.

Should students be required to participate in live video chats or record themselves? The only issue I have with this question is the word "required." Some students thrive on the attention and interaction with their classes in video chat. They look forward to it all day. For others, it's a nightmare. They don't want to show the conditions in which they live. They are insecure of how they look or sound, especially in their second language. Their technology skills are still developing and they have anxiety about participating in something like this.

If teachers would like to include video chat during virtual instruction, here are some suggestions:

- Do not require students to activate their microphone or camera all of the time. Students can actively participate through the chat feature if needed. If they are simply listening, this is absolutely a time in which they are gaining language through receptive means. I often do not require cameras during whole group instruction, but rather only in breakout rooms or smaller groups so I can better interact with them. Microphones are used during attendance in which all students respond with some sort of greeting

("Good morning!" "Hello." "How are you?") that was different from what they used the day prior. I then model the appropriate response to the greeting and students hear this several times over the class.

- Small-group chats are great ways to include our SLIFE and MLs. Melissa shares: ***"I have seven ELs spread out among my five classes. I set up a Google Classroom just for them with small-group meetings in which they seem to feel more comfortable talking. They still share on other platforms with their respective classes and are still part of those communities, but they have something that is safe and just for them."*** As long as our SLIFE and MLs are still 100% included in their class activities, adding another space for them may be an effective way to engage them in an additional way.
- Some platforms allow students to use subtitles during the meet. This may help students understand what is being said by hearing and reading the words, even if the words are all in English.
- Providing key vocabulary before video chats can help MLs build schema about the language that may be used or even prepare something to say ahead of time if they like.
- Reading books to students when they simply have to listen and watch is a great way to engage all in video chats, no matter the age of the students. Bonus points if it's reading for pleasure and not for an assessment!
- We've had some experiences with science in which students were asked to do experiments with items that (it was hoped) they had in their houses. Unfortunately, some of our students are renters and did not have access to parts of the house or items that would help them test out these theories. However, if the teacher were to do this while on video chat, she can model the experiments and describe and discuss

> what is happening. Science learning + language input = Win for SLIFE and MLs

A major concern during times of school closure is also access to food. By law, schools are still required to provide food to those who typically qualify for free/reduced lunch. However, ensuring that all families who would benefit from programs such as these know about their opportunities is the responsibility of the whole school community. Some districts had access to food scheduled at the same time as synchronous sessions of students' classes, which created a conflict for some families. Access to healthcare is also a great concern and something that may be more difficult with the closure of school.

During school closures, families have a variety of individual challenges. Some families have members who are unemployed and struggling financially. Others have parents who are working extra shifts to keep their jobs and put food on the table. Some are separated by social distancing rules. Family members may be sick or in the hospital. With these (and more!) in mind, our students may be taking on more responsibilities for care of siblings or older family members while still being expected to toe the line in school.

The moral of the story is: Be flexible. Be patient. Be understanding. Be supportive.

Assessments

Assessment during remote instruction is an extremely hot topic. Should students who are actively engaged and trying hard get the same grade as those who do not do anything? Should students who understand and apply what they've learned get assessed the same way as those who don't or cannot? Does it matter? What is the purpose of assessment? Is it a reward for good behavior or a punishment for not doing work? Is it used to inform instruction? Is it to compare student achievement among groups? Is it to provide feedback? The importance of assessment is so ingrained in our academic culture that it is difficult for us to pinpoint the reasons why education is so attached to this notion.

The basis of our educational system as it has been for years is assessment. **Did someone really learn something if it was never assessed??** (Yes! It happens every day!) With this change in "scenery" of education, assessment can be viewed in ways that we've never thought of before.

Some districts moved to a Pass/Fail assessment for report cards, and others deemed a 65 the lowest grade one can earn, whether or not the student participated. Some states cancelled standardized tests. Alternate ways of placement in ESL and other programs were established.

Some students view assessments as feedback of how well or poorly they are doing. They will use that feedback as encouragement to study certain areas better or that they understood well. It's ingrained in them as a part of school. Without formative assessments, some students are unsure and unsteady in terms of their work. With that being said, assessments during this time period—or any time period!—should only be formative and NOT punitive. We should be getting feedback on things with which students need assistance, rather than collecting data for them to fail. There are just too many variables going on that affect the instruction and their understanding of concepts.

During this time, teachers wonder if it is appropriate to give assessments, when students can simply look up answers and earn perfect scores. If this is a concern, then the type of assessment must change. If teachers are assessing students in ways that would be so basic as to allow them to Google the answer, we are doing something wrong. If a student can Google the answer to the question and then use that information to *apply* the knowledge, that can still be a valid assessment whether on virtual instruction or physically in the school. As our means of instructing students has had to undergo massive changes, so has our mindsets around assessing them.

If assessments were focused on showing students what they have accomplished during this time of remote instruction and how much they have achieved, this is a crucial assessment. There is a lot of frustration, questioning of ability, and uncertainty that students are experiencing. Many conversations have focused on what we have learned about assessments and growth during these times and how we will use this knowledge moving forward. We are now examining assessment and finding what never has worked...and what we can change for the future.

Goals of assessment should be to engage students in learning as authentically as possible. This is non negotiable.

Reflection discussion:

Reflection 1: As reluctant as I am to admit it, my home is not always "company ready" (I can picture my sisters laughing at this as they are reading this). If my boss were to arrive at my house with a film crew unannounced, I would be mortified and want to slam the door shut. I would like people invited into my home on my own terms and when I am prepared.

I find that this is how some of our students feel when forced to show themselves while in a video chat, particularly my middle schoolers. They do not like to show their faces, or even use their voices, during these chats. I later realized that some of them do not want to invite us all into their house. Some live in one room with several family members in a shared house. Some do not want to show their surroundings because they feel they might not have as nice a home as their classmates. Families may be out of work and there may be a lot of stress in their house. Some are babysitting siblings or cooking meals while they are trying to pay attention to a video chat. Maybe they are insecure with how they look themselves.

The thing is that we just don't know what our students' worries are. To require them to show their surroundings and themselves when they are uncomfortable is not culturally responsive or supportive.

Reflection 2: A teacher whom I knew years ago struggled with infertility. She worked at a religious school and knew that infertility treatments were not outwardly accepted by her employer (and some of her colleagues). She knew that this was the way that she was going to build her family, so she went ahead with treatments and chose to keep things quiet at work. She now is the proud mama to two beautiful children.

A former colleague of mine is a transgender woman who was a teacher. She lives her life as a strong, confident woman, but at the time did not choose to share her story with her employer, colleagues, or students. She later told her story publicly when she was ready and later became a well-known, confident LGBTQIA+ advocate.

Both of these women embrace their stories and lives wholeheartedly, but chose at the time not to share everything about them with their schools. I respect both of them and both of their stories, and I also respect their choices about with whom they share their lives. Everyone has their reasons for opening up about things, as do our students. When we thrust ourselves into the private world of our students' homes virtually, teachers must be sensitive to their individual situations and what they would willingly want to share with the world. This includes video chats, journals, and anything that is in a public forum.

Now that educators and parents are both more familiar with remote learning, we can now ensure that we create an environment in which all students are learning and progressing in a way in which they feel they belong. We now have accepted that this may be something that may happen again (or regularly) and we have to have a plan. Schools must now be ready within a day's notice to return to remote instruction at any point, whether it is to replace in-person instruction because of inclement weather or longer-term spans in which school buildings must be closed.

11

THE "WHOLE" CHILD

The challenges and failures of today do not define us, but what we do to overcome them paves the way to our success in the future.

Reflection questions:

- Is there an experience in your own life that changed the trajectory of your future? Do you ever wonder how your life would be different if this event hadn't happened?
- Can you think of a time in your life in which the journey was more important than the destination? Or vice versa?

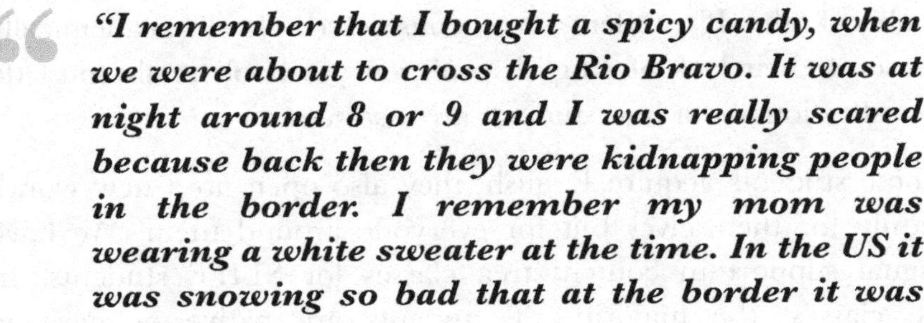

"I remember that I bought a spicy candy, when we were about to cross the Rio Bravo. It was at night around 8 or 9 and I was really scared because back then they were kidnapping people in the border. I remember my mom was wearing a white sweater at the time. In the US it was snowing so bad that at the border it was

> ***really cold. My mom—we were walking in the dark only her and me I was scared. I was only 10-years-old and then we saw a lot of black cars and my mom and me had to hide, but then we saw the ICE car and they got us. They brought us to the jail of immigrants, the ICE police had to check us. I had my favorite blanket with me and my candies. They took my blanket but the ICE police didn't take my candies away."***

Language differences—a challenge but also a benefit

Clearly, the most obvious challenge that is visible with our Newcomers is the language difference. (***"I try very hard and maybe people don't know that because they don't understand me"***—translated.) People often feel that not being able to speak English at all may be an insurmountable obstacle, but time and opportunity are often all that is needed for them to acquire English. Not knowing English is temporary for them; being multilingual will last them a lifetime.

Teachers may have to be reminded that Newcomers (even if they are SLIFE) are **not** blank slates. Although they may not have the English to show you how much they know, they certainly have been learning their whole lives. This may have been academic learning in schools or learning about the world through their life experiences—or most probably both. If students are considered "low" academically because of their lack of English proficiency, schools really must do some reflection about how students are assessed.

As these students acquire English, they also open up a new world, not only for themselves but for everyone around them. We have bilingual support in content-area classes for SLIFE students. In those classes, the majority of students are native or heritage speakers of Spanish, however, everyone benefits. Non-ESL students who speak Spanish have reported that hearing the support in Spanish helps reiterate to them the lesson, leading to greater understanding. Non-Spanish-speaking students report that they often still pay attention to the Spanish clarifications and find that they are trying to see if they understand, again getting the content twice (even if it's only part of it). These are global citizens, whether or not they are bilingual at this point. No longer will people be "annoyed" by the prompt to "Press 1 for English"; rather, encountering many languages and cultures is the norm for these young people.

SES (Socio-Economic Status) considerations

When Newcomers arrive, sometimes jobs are uncertain (or parents may have many jobs), living arrangements are tight, and there are many mouths to feed. I often find that our 8th graders have jobs to help contribute to the family and younger students are often in charge of younger siblings after school while their parents are working. ***"When I returned home from my job at 10 p.m., everyone was asleep and I was too tired to do my homework. I promise I'll try harder."*** If ever I feel as a teacher and parent that I don't get a break, I think of those children, with jobs or who are helping to raise younger siblings while still trying to be successful in school. The expectations may weigh heavily on their shoulders and we educators must understand that.

Food insecurity is very real for some students, Newcomers or not. Some families, despite the fact that they struggle to put food on the table, are reluctant to register for assistance (or free/reduced lunch) for a variety of reasons. These students sometimes face real hunger, which affects attention span, motivation, strength, and effort while we are working with them. The physical effects one feels when hungry are compounded by the SEMH (Social Emotional Mental

Health) effects that accompany not knowing when one's next meal may be.

In some districts there are uniforms, but in others, clothing and accessories may be a signal that students do not have money to spare. This can sometimes cause students to stick out if they "look like" they don't fit in with the other students. Students may sometimes have clothes that are old or worn out because they are given to them by someone else. For some students, these worries are on their minds constantly and color all interactions that they have with others throughout their day.

When it's the first winter in a new place, sometimes our families are not prepared for the cold. Several students reported seeing one of our Newcomers giving his jacket to his little brother while walking to school. We were able to ensure that he had a jacket appropriate for cold weather, but these students were offering to have a bake sale or even check their own houses for a jacket to fit him and keep him warm. One student remembered when she received a jacket from the school when her family couldn't purchase them a few years ago and wanted to be sure that our little Newcomer had the same opportunity. "Paying it forward" at its best.

Newcomers may come to us with enough life experiences to last, well, a lifetime. Others, however, do not have the opportunities that we generally think are essential to building schema and background for learning and it may be due to SES concerns. These types of experiences may include going to the zoo, museums, aquariums, or other types of learning excursions. Visits to the local community college or watching local theater also would build schema and give different perspectives for students about possibilities for them.

Missing family, past trauma, SEMH

In many countries around the world right now, schools are experiencing an influx of students who are leaving their homelands for reasons we cannot fathom or understand. These students may have experienced **trauma**, **loss**, **extreme poverty**, **lack of education**, **violence**, **threats**, or so many other horrors that may have caused them to leave or flee. Other students may enter our countries as **UMs** (Unaccompanied Minors) or may have reluctantly **left loved ones** (even immediate family) behind. When we recognize the journeys that some of these families undertake to reach their destinations, we realize the extreme amounts of stress involved!

When these students enter our classes, many teachers may only see their academic or linguistic needs. However, support for the loss or trauma that many of these students have experienced may be of more crucial importance. Although teachers are certainly not all certified SEMH (Social Emotional Mental Health) experts, there are many ways we can support these students who are entering our classrooms. According to Winokur (2020):

> *Social and Emotional Learning (SEL) and trauma-informed teaching are vital for us to ensure that all students learn, and that begins by helping them feel a sense of belonging in a safe space. They need to believe in their own self-worth before they can make a personal connection with their teacher and be on a path to personal wellbeing. Belonging Before Bloom (p. 85).*

Much like our student whom we lost, O, our students have so much that they carry on their shoulders that would be nearly impossible for many adults we know. ***"I wish they understand the problems I have in my life."*** Acknowledging that they may be juggling many challenges or emotions concerning their past experiences—in addition to adjusting to a new life—is extremely useful in terms of providing these students what they may need.

Counselors and psychologists who can communicate with these students are key to helping them through these SEMH issues. Teachers who support the students must be cognizant of signs that they are struggling emotionally or in fear, but understand that teachers cannot do it alone. Reaching out to specialists who can communicate with students and their families is the most important thing teachers can do to support these students. As we all recognize, it *does* take a village to meet the needs of a child.

But that doesn't mean that teachers do not play an essential role in the lives of these children. Sometimes they just need the opportunity to exhale. Providing a safe environment in the classroom can go a long way in helping students become acclimated to their new home, while also mending the wounds of the past. Teachers are in the position to support the SEMH of students within the scope of their "natural environment" rather than a clinical setting. The better our teachers are prepared to provide that supportive environment for our students, the healthier everyone will be (including the teachers!). Learning ways to be culturally responsive and respectful of students' struggles outside of school makes the weight on their shoulders all that much lighter for them.

Missing time/academics in school

We have been working hard to bridge the gaps of SLIFE who have missed periods of school before arriving. The "solution" for each student is as individual as the child. However, there are also times when we find that our students miss school for a variety of reasons after they are already with us.

One of the main reasons that I have found that students miss school when they are not sick is to care for a sibling while their parents are at work. One of my struggling fifth-graders kept missing school every time his sister stayed home sick because their parents had nowhere else to turn when she was home. When we discussed this with their parents, they replied that they would try to keep his younger sister healthier so both children would miss school less; they were not able to take off from work. I am certainly not criticizing these parents (as frustrated as I may have felt on behalf of our student!). As a working mother, I understand the predicament in which they found themselves.

Appointments for the family is another reason that students may miss school. As they are making gains with their understanding and use of English, their parents need their help with legal and medical matters. Most of these offices are open during school hours, so it is often necessary for students to miss school to translate for their families.

Unfortunately, sometimes our students are missing school because of behavior problems. Either they are avoiding school and the mental and physical exhaustion that they experience, or they are getting in trouble for a variety of reasons. Think of the student discussed in Chapter 2 whose family fled their country to escape gangs; there are so many challenges that these students may have after the trauma they have experienced. These struggles may result in poor peer relations, resistance to following authority, difficulty with anger management, lack of motivation, and a host of other issues. We are not always in the position to "fix" everything for any of our students, but maintaining a supportive environment as much as possible for these students is imperative.

Sarah discussed the situation that she encountered with her Newcomer who came as a seventh grader. Although his daily attendance was good, he missed class every time he had an outburst—which was often several times a day. He would snap or shove someone or something whenever there was a slightest conflict or if a teacher put any sort of academic or behavioral demand on him. He growled and paced the floor, yelling in Spanish. Teachers assumed he was cursing or threatening and he likely was. Teachers and the guidance counselor called him the "Raging Bull" and because of his behavior, he was constantly removed from class to be sent to the classroom in which she was teaching. Sarah would allow him space to calm down and then he would go to his next class. Although this certainly was not ideal and it is absolutely the school's responsibility to have more supports in place for students like this, he was given his "safe space" with a teacher with whom he had a connection to calm down. Sarah reports seeing him working in town at a restaurant while in high school—and speaking to her completely in English (and with pride in his voice!).

Safety/security/bullying/politics

Some families move several times without settling for long. Other families are very vested in their new town and hope with all they have that they have settled in the place that is right for them. Either way, feeling uncertain about one's family's security takes a toll on the entire family, including the children. Whether or not documentation is an issue for our Newcomers, there is often a feeling of nervousness or unease as they settle into their new home. Families coming from other countries may have come from a place that is dramatically different from their destination. Do they lock their doors? Are children safe outside unsupervised? Are police helpful or corrupt? Are the schools welcoming and supportive? Can we trust anyone?

New neighbors are not always welcomed with open arms in all communities. Sometimes there are preconceived notions about certain populations or possibly bad experiences in the past that cause resentments that greet our Newcomers. ***"I want that Americans know that Mexicans are very nice. They are generous and we lived in very beautiful places."*** It is difficult when you arrive in a situation in which you later realize that you are not wanted.

I think that there are many political (local and otherwise) reasons why people are reluctant to have our Newcomers come into town. Among them is the way that some schools are funded: by local taxes. People see families move into town, assume that they will need services in the schools, and resent the "strain on the local economy" that these families represent. There are also political issues in terms of immigrants entering our country about which people feel very strongly on all sides. The bottom line is that these are children who, once here, are entitled to an education. Investing in these children is investing in the future of our community.

Families often have these discussions in front of their children and this sometimes manifests into problems in school. If the children feel that they have more of a "right" to be somewhere than someone else, that could be a basis of uneven power in relationships and problems in the classroom. This could happen between students who have grown up in the community and Newcomers...or be among Newcomers. Tolerance and respect are taught in the home, and "dinner table talk" will make its way into school one way or another.

Friendships and relationships

Much like with other students, friendships for Newcomers may be complex. Teachers and administrators often assume who would be friends with Newcomers based upon factors that we see: common languages, time spent together in class, or similar backgrounds. Very often, this is a solid foundation for friendship, but other times there are other variables involved.

Sometimes they are the only ones in the class or group who speak their primary language and it is very difficult to get beyond superficial interactions without a common language. ***"I like being friends but speaking with them is hard for me"***—translated. However, if teachers intentionally create collaborative groups with Newcomers paired with students who do not speak the language (yet who are patient, kind and welcoming), wonderful things can happen. Addison was so excited to become friends with a Newcomer that they drew pictures, giggled and played together on the playground...all while learning words in each other's languages. Another Newcomer was so interested in becoming friends with a boy in his class who didn't speak Spanish that he would enlist another friend as a translator...and they all played together and a friendship blossomed for the three of them. Two of our seventh graders would walk home from school together using the translate feature on their phones to communicate and connect, laughing the whole way.

If there are groups of Newcomers who speak the same language, this can be both a blessing and a challenge. We have groups of girls or boys who stick together—perhaps out of necessity, perhaps because they share the same classes, perhaps because they enjoy each other's company. Under good circumstances, they provide one another support, share common experiences, and make it so no one is ever alone or left out. Other times, it may be that these students prefer other people and someone is left out or that they simply do not get along. ***"Miss, I don't know what I did wrong. They don't talk to me anymore"***—translated. As a human being, it breaks my heart to see someone alone in the cafeteria or hallways, and we always work to ensure that this is not the case. It's easy to assume that these students who are experiencing this transition at the same time should be besties—and when it works out it's great—but it's not always the case.

Students who are older also have the added challenge of relationships beyond friendships. While language can certainly be an obstacle, cultural differences may also play a part. ***"It's weird when my friends are dating. I'm not interested in that. My family will arrange my marriage and if I date someone they think it will be for marriage."*** Jessica's student mentioned to other Newcomers that he is gay and they responded with laughter. He came to Jessica devastated that the other students in his Newcomer class wouldn't accept him for who he is. A different view on relationships is sometimes a difference that a young person will take to heart, and understanding the importance of that is key to connecting with and supporting him.

Possible undiagnosed learning disabilities

There is a lot of debate when one of our MLs shows unusually difficult struggles while still acquiring the English language. It is a very real, very valid question to wonder if these struggles are a result of a learning disability/problem or a language acquisition issue. If a student is considered a SLIFE, this complicates things all the more. While certainly there are students who have learning disabilities in every part of our population, one must be sure to consider all of the needs and challenges of all learners before determining that they may have a disability. So, there are several things to think about; however, any one of them may not be an indicator of a learning disability.

- What exactly are the concerns? Do they transcend different areas of the student's day? For example, does the child have difficulties in math versus literacy versus unstructured classroom/hallway time? Do the parents report concerns at home that mirror school issues?
- Are the concerns specific to unmastered skills that are specific to previous grades?
- Has the child's hearing and vision been checked by the school nurse? (being cautious not to require children to identify letters or read to indicate ability to see/hear)
- Does the child lack self-awareness? This may be perceived as spatial-visual difficulties, little awareness of body space, volume in speaking, and other ways.
- Are the concerns dominant-language based? Does the student have difficulties following directions or

communicating in his dominant language? Does the student have problems with literacy in his dominant language? How are these challenges assessed?

- Are the concerns based upon the acquisition of the target language? How long has the student been learning in English? If literacy or communication in the target language is the concern, are there issues consistent with second language acquisition?
- Have intervention-type services been provided? What is the nature of the intervention? Has data been collected?
- Is the child showing feelings of being upset or frustrated with oneself?
- Are there problems "across the board" with other students that may indicate there is an issue with Tier 1 instruction or availability of services for students overall? Are the Tier 1 programs appropriate for learners who may be multilingual?

Although there certainly may be students who are struggling in our classes, we must make a differentiation between learning *difficulties* and learning *disabilities*. Learning difficulties may come from missed education, lack of language development or support at home, or any number of other needs that have not been met. These may stem more from *a lack of opportunity* than a special education issue. Learning disabilities, on the other hand, are measured on assessments as the difference between a student's potential and the student's actual abilities.

We also have long-term MLs who have many struggles with their learning. We have to examine the accessibility of services that they had over their years in the district, in addition to analyzing where their problems were over the years. In terms of how quickly (or slowly) our students are learning English, one must remember: Learning a different language is not easy under the best of circumstances! And, honestly, some of our students are not learning under great circumstances.

Language or literacy difficulties and their effect on SEMH

Frustrations with challenges that come with being new to a country and not knowing the language may cause problems for some families. Sometimes the difficulties are so overwhelming that it may seem that there is no light at the end of the tunnel.

> ***"I like the teacher to know the students think I can't do anything and they tell the teacher I can't speak English. I can do things but not everything. I am not stupid I just need learn more English."***

By encouraging a growth mindset, our Newcomers (and their families and teachers!) can focus on the possibilities of the future rather than the frustrations of the present. A growth mindset is one in which one sees that hard work and perseverance will make a difference for oneself in life, rather than the current difficulties being the future. The challenges and failures of today do not define us, but what we do to overcome them paves the way to our success in the future.

Students who come with little knowledge of English can feel so overwhelmed by the daunting task of learning. ***"I want to learn more English so I can talk to others. And I want to have less shame when I am talking"***—translated. Older students, in particular, have this self-consciousness when speaking in the target language, especially in front of their peers. They feel that their mistakes in language production indicate that they are stupid or unable to learn. What they don't realize, however, is that those mistakes are a roadmap to becoming a bilingual person, which is a huge asset.

Literacy is a hurdle for many of our Newcomers, whether or not they have literacy in their dominant language. There are so many emotions that are attached to difficulties with literacy. Ensuring that we meet our Newcomers' needs (in terms of reading, but also emotionally) is crucial to helping them progress. Finding students where they are and working with them at that level nonjudgmentally with their dignity in mind is critical for their success and well being.

Keeping a student's SEMH in mind is critical in ensuring that we do our due diligence in obtaining the correct level of services for them. We most certainly do not want a child to be classified as needing special education services erroneously; conversely, pushing children along without providing them with the services they need is setting them up for failure.

Ensuring that all assessments and evaluations are valid and culturally appropriate is absolutely essential to meeting the needs of all students. If we are faithfully using assessments as means to better understand the needs of our students, they cannot be "one size fits all" or have bias towards specific populations. Often these assessments assume life experiences that our students may not have had (riding the bus to school, Thanksgiving celebrations, assumptions about families or living situations).

To be clear, students should not be precluded from being assessed for special education based on their status as English learners. Every student is as individual as his or her needs. However, there should be a protocol for determining the propriety of this route, as well as other documented interventions that are appropriate to the language differences of these children.

Exceptionality

Just as statistics show that some of our Newcomers may have learning difficulties, we must acknowledge that some may be gifted academically. Lynette describes her experience with one of her students from her first year of teaching:

"I'll never forget Abraham. Abraham was always on the ball. He knew most answers before I even had the chance to ask the questions. There was something very special about Abraham. He was performing at remarkably high levels when compared to his peers. He was incredibly curious and motivated. I believed he was gifted. I tried so hard to get him G&T services but the system just didn't provide services for students who only spoke Spanish. It was so sad to me that a smart child like this wasn't able to have the same opportunities other children were able to have. Just because he didn't know the language didn't mean he wasn't entitled to the same services. As much as I pushed for G&T services, it didn't matter. I felt frustrated. It wasn't fair. The year went on and I tried my best to differentiate for Abraham as much as I could. The year ended and he moved on to second grade. About five years later I found out he was actually transferred to one of the gifted and talented schools. At that point, he knew English well. I never forgot about Abraham. He was brilliant. Just one of those students that you never forget." Lynette's student came to visit her 12 years later. *"You were my favorite teacher and I will never forget all you did for me. I came here today to tell you that I was accepted into medical school,"* he said. Lynette recalls, *"It was a wonderful moment. I was proud to say that I maybe had made a difference at some point in his life. I believe that all students in this country should have the same opportunities. Maybe if Abraham would have gotten gifted and talented services earlier on, his education would have been accelerated at an earlier stage in his life. Maybe it would have made more of a difference."*

Lynette's powerful story is a reminder that there must be equity for all students, including opportunities for placement in advanced or higher-level classes if possible. Just because students may not speak English as their first language does not mean that they should be excluded from educational opportunities. They are absolutely entitled.

Inconsistency with medical care

Knowledge of the healthcare system in a new country can be very tricky for many people. Let's face it, maneuvering insurance is often tricky for all of us. However, there may not be consistent benefits, work, or doctors for our Newcomer families and that can be extremely problematic at times. Copays and out-of-pocket expenses may also become obstacles to medical care. If families do not drive, going to doctors or specialists out of town may be difficult as well.

Maria and Michelle found that their little kinder Newcomer was limping for weeks after a fall on the playground. His mother brought him to the pediatrician—at their suggestion—a number of times as the weeks went by. Mom was beginning to get annoyed with the teachers, but finally took their advice and followed up with a specialist, which was no small feat. The pediatric specialist was about a half-hour away by car, and this family had to work out taking a cab, as they did not have transportation. Unfortunately, this specialist found a tumor growing on the bone of the afflicted leg, which was causing the pain for our little guy. ***"We just knew something just wasn't right."*** Because of the persistence and attention of his teachers, this little guy is now in third grade and doing much better.

Another parent of a Newcomer reports that she found out immediately after she sent for her 6-year-old son to come to live with her in the United States that she herself had cancer. ***"I didn't have support and didn't know what to do to get treatment for myself while not letting my son know what was going on. I didn't want to scare him"***—translated. Sometimes that support system that one has when they live near family and friends isn't there when they move to a different country, even if they have been there for years.

Mental health is a facet of healthcare that many do not understand how to navigate. This type of care is something crucial that some may just avoid because they do not know how to access it. Also, many of our families find that they are living in "crisis mode" in which they take care of problems that they cannot avoid as they arise. Many cultures also place a stigma on this type of illness. Mental health problems may not be as "immediate" looking like a broken arm, but advocates must help these families care for themselves both inside and out.

Different norms in school/community

Our students arriving from other countries into our districts may have had a completely different experience in school prior to coming to us. Some refer to a one-room schoolhouse that encompassed all of the grades (***"I can't believe the fifth grade has its own room!"*** —translated), and others had classrooms outside because there weren't buildings specifically for schools in their countries. To assume that these students would know our "unwritten" rules or norms would make life very difficult for them. ***"I'm not rude, I just don't understand"***—translated.

At times, Newcomers do not understand the norms that other students have grown up with...and it's easy for teachers to feel frustrated with this. Calling out, talking while the teacher is teaching, and difficulties while working collaboratively all are things that may have to be explicitly taught for the student to know to avoid. As students get more comfortable with being in their new classroom, they may remember the experiences they associate with their previous times in school, which may have looked very different.

Inconsistent housing or homelessness

If the security or continuity of one's home is not there, it may be unreasonable for that person to concentrate or even "hold it together" behaviorally as one would typically expect. ***"We moved again and I still do not have a mattress. I'm sleeping on the floor and my neck and my back hurt. There are bed bugs from the people before us*** [shows bug bites]***. I am having a bad day."*** When families come to a new country and are still settling, it can certainly take a toll on the children. Some families may find that the housing that they counted on isn't working and then do not have a place to stay.

What does that mean for the teachers of these students? Sometimes students (or parents) do not share this information, but when they are ready to let you know something like this, you must spring into action. What resources are available locally for this student (either through the school or through the community)?

Parents with the inability to be involved—for a variety of reasons

Parents working multiple jobs or shifts that do not mirror the school day make it extremely difficult for them to support their children academically. If they arrive home late at night, there is little opportunity for them to read to their children or check their homework or monitor their academics. As much as they want to help their children succeed and as much as they value school, sometimes it is impossible for them to physically support them.

We as educators must be sure to leave the judgment aside when working to help these families. It is very easy to rest on one's own privilege to disparage the decisions and choices made by someone whose shoes we do not wear. It is crucial that we support these families as best we can with the help of our colleagues and community—it is an investment in their future.

Reflection discussion:

Reflection 1: When reflecting upon one's own life and the different twists and turns that we have experienced, sometimes there are times or decisions that change our lives, for better or for worse. For some, it may be decisions having to do with the college one attended or the person one married. Others may look to a tragedy, like the loss of a parent, when they think of a life-changing moment for them. Perhaps yet others remember buying the winning ticket for the lottery as their pivotal change in their lives!

However, for our students, a major change in the trajectory of their lives may be the move to a new country. Nothing will ever be the same again, whether or not they eventually return. Much like our reflections on our lives, this change may be a representation of both positive changes and things that cause them to feel grief and loss.

Teachers may sometimes impose their own views on the circumstances of Newcomers as they arrive in their classrooms. *"He's so lucky that he is here now." "His life will be so much better than it was." "He has so many new opportunities here that he would not have had."* Yet, how the student feels may be completely different—and may change depending upon the day. Acknowledging and understanding the very unique experiences of our Newcomers and supporting them however they are handling their experiences is crucial to establishing positive relationships with them.

Reflection 2: When we have driven to Florida from our home in New Jersey, we have always wanted to drive as many miles as possible on the first day so the second day would be light and the destination will be close. Sometimes that means eating lunch in the car or getting up very early to start our trip then driving later into the night. Our friends Chris and Jill take a different approach. They decide that they will stop at the halfway point between New Jersey and Florida and they take their time on the ride down. They stop for a nice lunch and enjoy the ride. If they reach their destination in the late afternoon, then they stop at the hotel and enjoy the pool and maybe a glass of wine. For us, our vacation starts when we reach Florida. For Chris and Jill, their vacation started from the moment they left their home. Clearly, for them, the journey is an important part of the trip while we look at it as the means to our destination.

The journey that our students have taken to get to us—however they have come—is just as important as their destination. ***"I found myself on top of my dad walking through the humid air. I started walking and we swam through cool water that felt relaxing until we crossed the river. We went under a tunnel into the USA."*** Their experiences may have been exciting or it may have been terrifying. Their journeys may have been a quick airplane ride or a trip that lasted several weeks. Either way, it is part of the blueprint of their lives.

As we get to know the backgrounds of our students, we find that their experiences are as unique as they are. They all have a story to tell and a Voice to decide what their contribution to the world will be. As teachers, it is our responsibility to provide them the opportunity to use their Voice, however they choose to do so.

NEXT STEPS

We revisit the purpose of this book as outlined in the Introduction.

This book is meant to spark conversation and inspire creativity in working with MLs. There are discussion questions for each chapter that are designed to help us connect with the material and with our students. Our passion for teaching does not only include certain "flavors" of students; it must be extended to include children with a variety of backgrounds, SES, languages, abilities, and cultures. It is every teacher's responsibility to educate all students in their classes; some just need some support in how best to do so.

We cannot be afraid to advocate for our Newcomers and SLIFE, as we must for all of our students. Sometimes this advocacy is towards our administration, our local government, our community members...or our fellow teachers. We must focus on the assets of these children and what they contribute to the school community—even if these assets are not apparent yet. We have to encourage children to embrace their story and how it has made them who they are. They are in charge of their own story, their own voice. It is our responsibility to provide opportunities for literature and learning that open their eyes and build them up. When people believe in them, children internalize this and can achieve great things.

Mami dónde vamos I told her
She replied al otro lado
I didn't know what that was
So I just followed.
(by Jesús)

REFERENCES

Cummins, J. (2000) Second language teaching for academic success: A framework for school language policy development. Symposium, Stockholm, Sweden.

Cummins, J. (2007, January) Promoting literacy in multilingual contexts. Ontario: The Literacy and Numeracy Secretariat.

Cummins, J. (2018, April) Jim Cummins on language teaching methods and translanguaging. https://www.youtube.com/watch?v=D-lBiQyA1Fs

Cummins, J. (2020) Reading and the English language learner: Instructional implications of the research evidence. Webinar: Pearson PreK-12.

Garcia Mathewson, T. (2016, June 23) Signing ESSA in law was only the beginning. *K-12 Dive. https://www.k12dive.com/news/signing-essa-into-law-was-only-the-beginning/421311/*

Krashen, S., & Terrell, T. (1983) *The Natural Approach*. Prentice Hall.

Krashen, S. (2019, April 17) Beginning reading. *Language Magazine, Improving Literacy and Communication.* https://www.languagemagazine.com/2019/04/17/beginning-reading/

Krisnaswami, U. (2019, January 17) Why stop at mirrors and windows? Children's books prisms. https://www.hbook.com/?detailStory=why-stop-at-windows-and-mirrors-childrens-bookprisms

Ladson-Billings, G. (1995). Toward a theory of culturally relevant pedagogy. *American educational research journal*, *32*(3), 465-491.

Logan, J. (2019) When children are not read to at home. *Journal of Developmental and Behavioral Pediatrics.* https://www.sciencedaily.com/releases/2019/04/190404074947.htm

Kaufman, S.B. (2020) Who created Maslow's iconic pyramid? https://scottbarrykaufman.com/who-created-maslows-iconic-pyramid/

McLeod, S. (2020) Maslow's Hierarchy of Needs. www.simplypsychology.org

Salva, C., & Matis, A. (2017). *Boosting achievement: Reaching students with interrupted or minimal learning.* Seidlitz Education.

Style, E. (1988) Curriculum as a window and mirror. *Listening for All Voices*. Oak Knoll School Monograph.

Winokur, I. (2020) Belonging before Bloom, Not Maslow before Bloom. In S. Thomas (Ed.), *Snapshot in Education 2020* (pp. 77-94). EduMatch Publishing.

Vygotsky, L.S. (1978) *Mind in society: The development of higher psychological processes.* Harvard University Press.

APPENDIX

Unpacking the suitcase...

Newcomers bring with them life experiences that can support (or challenge!) their academic success with us. Understanding what is in their "suitcase" of experiences can help us meet their needs. The following is a list of things to consider when thinking of the "whole child."

SLIFE?

Reasons for relocation?

Family separation?

Age when arrived?

Literacy of parents?

Aptitude for learning?

Familiarity with technology?

Support system for family?

Responsibilities at home?

Trauma?

Literacy experiences in dominant language?

Motivation?

Siblings?

SES?

Attitude towards school?

Previous exposure to English?

Feelings of permanency?

Social-Emotional Mental Health?

Home Language Survey Questions:

Feel free to use any or all of these questions. Parents should answer the starred questions only if comfortable. Having these surveys available in the languages of the families is crucial, even if the translation is done electronically.

What language(s) are spoken in the home by your child? Are there other languages spoken in the home?

What are the ways in which the school can contact home or family members?

What is the country of origin of your family?

What grades have your child completed? Has there been any time elapsed since he or she last attended school?

What type of school did your child attend?

Are there any adults who understand or read English in the home/family?

*Are there any medical concerns for your child?

*Parent commentary of student's experience with learning/schools

*Does your child have concerns or worries about school?

Introductory Activities

The following is a working list of activities to do in order to immediately help our Newcomers acclimate to our school and things to keep in mind during the first days. Based on the individual needs of each student, some activities may be necessary and others may not.

- Be sure the student has a folder or paper with their name and classroom number/teacher on it with them at all times. Allow the student to write this information themself and practice asking for and responding with this information in English. This can help the student answer questions about who they are and where they belong if they get flustered.
- Ensure the student understands procedures for leaving the room (bathroom, nurse, drink) and that it's ok to ask. Actually walk the student to the nurse to introduce him so they understand what the office looks like, even if they don't remember how to get there.
- Go over lunch procedures and make sure the student has a code. If snacks are eaten in class, make sure the student knows what's acceptable to bring. Ask some friendly students to help them in the cafeteria if necessary.
- Provide the student with an opportunity to write about something about themself in their native language or with any English they know. This can provide you with much insight to our Newcomer's experiences or information about them. Use Google translate if necessary to read it.
- Translanguaging (switching between languages) is a valid phase in language acquisition. Please allow students to leverage their native language in order to acquire English.
- Uniforms, beginning/end times, arrival/dismissal procedures all need to be explained.
- Snow days/emergency closings and how to get the information must be explained if applicable.
- Go over different types of emergency drills and be sure to give support or assign a peer buddy during them (may trigger past traumas).
- Obtain passwords/computer access as soon as possible and show them Google translate or other useful sites to help empower students with a means of communication. Students may or may not have computer skills. If handheld translators are available, teach students how to use it.
- Native language literacy skills assessments are helpful if available. Don't assume our newcomers have on-level literacy skills, but whatever skills they already have can be used to develop skills in English.

Checklist for Choosing Quality Literature for MLs

	Is this quality literature? Think of themes being important to the students, if the writing is rich and detailed, and the characters are solid. Is this book/poetry/short story worth your (and their) time?
	Would this book be a window, mirror, or sliding door to my students?
	Are diverse cultures authentically represented in this literature?
	Is the book's vocabulary meaningful for use today? Or is it full of outdated jargon that would not benefit the students to learn?
	Would this book help build the schema of my students in different areas? Books that help give information that may be useful in different aspects of students' lives will give them more "bang for their buck."
	Are the characters well developed and are there ways for students to relate to them? Does the voice of the character resonate with my students?
	Can my students learn from the conflict and resolution and possibly apply those skills in their own lives?
	Are the themes universal?
	Is the story entertaining and engaging for my students' imaginations? Can I interact with my students creatively based on aspects of this literature? Will my students laugh?
	Does this represent a genre that is different from other books in the curriculum or classroom?
	Can this literature be juxtaposed with another piece of literature for the analysis of the students?

Tips for small-group ML instruction
Always begin with appropriate greetings in English and require that they respond and ask how you are! This engages the students with pleasantries with which this reinforcement may help them gain confidence and they can use the greetings with others.
Create a word ring of high-frequency words (choose words based on use-value). Start with two/three words and then add two words each time you meet. Time permitting: Review words daily, explain the meaning, and use them in sentences. As students get to know the words, they may be able to define, give examples or create sentences for the words. Ask the students to study them at home and bring them back to you each time you meet.
Work with a book. I like to use a mixture of quality literature (multicultural is great!) and books that feature high-frequency words or leveled readers. If you choose to use the books that are photocopies, you can have the students highlight high-frequency words or chunks/sound combinations that they recognize.
Have students attempt to read the books to themselves and you can listen to each in turn and provide support in decoding words. Remember: not every mistake must be corrected! Think about mistakes that are meaning-changing mistakes or words that are crucial that the student knows.
When finished reading, choose a picture or two (or all--depending upon the length of the book) to discuss. Talking about the pictures in books can allow students to make connections between the illustrations and new vocabulary.
Focus on positive interactions with books and fostering good experiences!!
Don't hesitate to ask questions or try new things! Any time students are working with books and in the target language, they are learning.

Following is a sample of tips to share with content-area teachers:

We have long felt it is a challenge to include our multilingual learners in the rest of our content-area classes. While nothing is "perfect," our goal is to give them as many opportunities to gain content knowledge—and experience the English language—as possible. We sincerely appreciate your dedication and hard work in differentiating your lessons to meet the needs of our multilingual learners.

- ★ Remember that **productive vocabulary** can sometimes develop much later than **receptive vocabulary** for our multilingual learners. In other words, students usually understand much more of the target language than they have the ability to speak or write. You may also find that students are unwilling or unable to participate in class discussions or are very quiet while in your class; this is a normal part of second language acquisition and hopefully, this will improve as they become more confident in the target language.
- ★ When possible, **read aloud** directions or information that you have **written** on the board for students so they have the opportunity to experience the language in both written and spoken modalities. Clarifying content-area words or using more common synonyms is very helpful.
- ★ Create a **"useful" vocabulary list** for each activity and allow students to translate words or phrases into their native language. They can use bilingual dictionaries or (if you have computer/iPad access) online translators. They can also translate simple questions on the topics and attempt to answer in English. Another option is for students to use the dictionaries or technology to find synonyms or pictures to help them master difficult content-area words in English. **Word mapping** is also a useful tool for students to use to really understand concepts with new or different vocabulary and is supported within the ELA curriculum.
- ★ Provide a **picture/visual** of the item or person who is connected to a key concept in your lesson to your MLs. They can create a list of adjectives in their native language and then translate to English as time permits. You can also direct them to make predictions or evaluations about the concept based on the picture.

- Provide opportunities for students to work with "**more knowledgeable peers**" (Vygostky) to help them understand concepts/directions. Not only would this help the ML, but this can bring the other student into the "target zone" (or a "4" in our learning scales for Marzano), where they are able to teach the concept to others. But be certain, though, not to put too much stress or responsibility on the "more knowledgeable" student; they must understand that their first priority is their own work, rather than assisting their classmates.
- If students are reading a passage in your class based on content-area material, your MLs can scan through the passage and identify "**cognates**" (words that are similar in English and another language). If students speak a language that shares cognates with English, they can be used to allow MLs to make inferences about the text without constantly translating. You can then allow them to hypothesize about the rest of the text. *Identifying cognates can also be useful for the teacher when looking at the result of student work.*
- There are several translating **websites** available to help students understand questions. They do not provide perfect translations, but can definitely help give the students an idea of a topic or task to complete. The students can also input their answers into the translator to help you determine if your students are understanding the key concepts of the assignment.
- As much as leveraging knowledge in our students' native language can be helpful in increasing vocabulary and understanding in the content areas, it is crucial to realize that some of our students (particularly at the elementary level) may not have well-developed literacy skills in their first language, for a variety of reasons. If you find this to be the case, focusing on **simplifying English vocabulary**, using pictures/charts/graphs or technology can help bridge the communication gap. Picture dictionaries are helpful, along with simplifying vocabulary. If you have a classroom library from which students can choose books, having low-level, high-interest books on various content-area topics can be a great way to get students engaged in the target language.
- Activate **background knowledge** throughout the lesson (books the class has

read, areas of the world studied...). This can also include any connections to the students' cultures, family situations, native countries, experiences.

★ Provide **visuals** to content vocabulary as much as possible. These may be videos, pictures, graphs, realia.
★ Engaging students in writing is crucial for language (and confidence!) development. For some students, this may manifest in paragraphs in their native language. Others may be able to use "**translanguaging**" techniques and provide writing that leverages both the target language and their native language. Yet we will have students in all grade levels who have not yet developed their writing skills. Allowing these students to draw images, circle answers, write lines to match information or any manner in which they can indicate their understanding or express themselves is important. Producing language at the "word" level, rather than the "sentence/phrase" level, is still a valid stage in language acquisition that allows students to utilize their skills in different modalities.

Sentence frames:

The characters' names are __________ and __________.

The setting is __________( ) and __________( ).

The conflict is between the _________________ and the colonists.

________ means to move to a new country.

Today is _______ (Month day, year)

In this timeline, ___________ is the event that happened *first* in the year _______. *After* this event, ______________ happened in the year _______.

_______ + _______ = ________ ________ < ________

Na + Cl = _____________ (____________). The color of ___________ is _____________, ___________ is used for __________.

The ________ is the center of the earth. It is made of _______ and ______.

If I could travel to ____________, I would see ___________.

My sister's name is _________ and she is _____ years old. She is _______, _______, and _______. She likes to _______. She lives in ________.

Sentence stems:

Two descriptions of the main character are...

The setting of this book is important because...

Three ways to describe myself are...

My favorite activity is...

The results of this experiment will show...

Last weekend, I...

Winter is better than summer because...

In my opinion...

According to the author...

In the future...

I solved this problem by...

Sample lesson plan

Essential question: What are the contributions of people who had unusual roles in the American Revolutionary War?

Content objective: Students will *research* about the contributions of women during the Revolutionary War.

Language objective: Students will *read* passages and *watch* a video about the contributions of women in the Revolutionary War. Students will *write* the information in a graphic organizer and *present* the information in a small group.

Frontloaded vocabulary:
contribution
Patriot
revolution
rights
taxes
government

Materials:
-Reading passages about Molly Pitcher and other women during the Revolutionary War
-YouTube video about women in the war (students may use subtitles in other languages if desired)
-Graphic organizer

Procedures/Activities:

1. Who are the people who are most often represented as making contributions during the American Revolutionary War in history books? Students will brainstorm other groups of people who may have contributed.
2. Read passages with information about various women who made contributions for the Patriots and their various reasons for doing so
3. Watch video about Women in the Revolution
4. Work collaboratively to complete a graphic organizer about women in the revolution
5. Present information about women in small groups

Adaptations:

ELs: frontloaded vocabulary, subtitles for video if needed, graphic organizers, passages with guided notes, sentence stems

Ss with IEPs/504s: passages with guided notes, graphic organizers

Formative assessments: graphic organizer; participation in presentations

Suggestions to Help Your Child with Reading

Your child should read at least 20 minutes each night.

Parents of students who are emergent readers: Please read together in whichever language and then talk about what you read.

Examples of questions you can ask after reading:

	Who are the main characters of the story? How are they important to the development of the story?
	Is this book fiction or nonfiction? How do you know?
	What is the setting of the story?
	What is the problem in the story? How is it resolved?
	From whose point of view is the story told? How do we know this?
	Does the main character learn a lesson during the story?
	What type of connection can you make to something in the story?
	What is the main idea of the story?
	How would this be different if it took place in a different time period?
	Summarize the action of the story in five sentences.
	Draw your favorite scene of the book.

	How is this story similar to another book you have read?
	How are you similar or different to a character in this story?
	What is your favorite part of the story? Why?
	What did you learn from this story?
	Would you change the ending of the story? How?
	Describe a picture that you saw in the book.

Sugerencias Para Ayudar a Su Hijo/a Con la Lectura

Su hijo/a debe leer por lo menos veinte minutos cada noche. Después de leer, hablen con su hijo/a de lo que leyó.

Padres de estudiantes que son lectores emergentes: Por favor, lean con su hijo/a en cualquier idioma cada noche. Cuando terminan, hablen de lo que han leído. Ejemplos de preguntas para los niños después de leer:

	¿Quiénes son los personajes principales de la historia? ¿Por qué son importantes en el desarrollo del cuento?
	¿Es esta historia de tipo ficción o no ficción? ¿Cómo sabes?
	¿En cuál lugar y tiempo está la historia?
	¿Cuál es el problema del cuento? ¿Cómo se resuelve?
	¿De cuál punto de vista es la historia? ¿Cómo sabes?
	¿El personaje principal aprende una lección durante la historia?
	¿Qué tipo de conexión puedes hacer con algo en esta historia?
	¿Cuál es la idea central (o principal) del cuento?
	¿Cómo será diferente esta historia durante otra época?
	Resume la acción de la historia en cinco oraciones.

	Dibuja tu escena favorita del libro.
	¿Cómo es esta historia similar a otro libro que has leído?
	¿Cómo eres similar o diferente que un personaje en esta historia?
	¿Cuál es tu parte favorita de la historia? ¿Por qué?
	¿Qué aprendiste en esta historia?
	¿Cambiarías el fin de la historia? ¿Cómo?
	Describe en tres oraciones un dibujo que ves en el libro.

Following is a sample pacing guide for a Newcomer curriculum:

ESL/Newcomer Curriculum Pacing Guide

Grade Level: 3 – 5

Unit Number / Theme Name	Unit Description	Timeline
Unit 1 - Myself	This unit is designed to engage the Newcomer in producing the target language while talking and writing about things that are important to him or her. Learners will acquire vocabulary associated with self-description, advocacy for oneself in the classroom, basic greetings, and first-person pronouns. Basic information about oneself is included, such as age, grade, parent phone number, and address. Informal and formal assessments of language and literacy will be done (if appropriate).	5-6 weeks in duration; May begin whenever Newcomers arrive
Unit 2 – My Family	This unit is designed to engage the Newcomer in producing the target language while talking and writing about things having to do with their family and/or culture. Learners will acquire vocabulary associated with family members, descriptions, third-person pronouns, and question words. (Content from Unit 1 will be spiraled within Unit 2.)	5-6 weeks
Unit 3 – My Community	This unit is designed to engage the Newcomer in producing the target language while talking and writing about things having to do with our community. Learners will acquire vocabulary associated with school, money, time, and vocabulary to use downtown. (Content from Units 1 & 2 will be spiraled within Unit 3.)	5-6 weeks
Unit 4 – My World	This unit is designed to engage the Newcomer in producing the target language while talking and writing about things having to do with the world. Learners will acquire vocabulary associated with current events, literature, and using the internet. Learners will also research and write about issues from their native country. (Content from Units 1, 2 & 3 will be spiraled within Unit 4.)	6-7 weeks

Create routines that help scaffolding. What is scaffolding? Scaffolds are ways that teachers can support students (like the scaffolding on a building) to help them engage in work that may be too challenging for them to complete. Teachers must be sure to not provide more help than students need, but enough to meet their needs.

- → Restating, Paraphrasing
- → Wait time
- → Graphic organizers
- → Outlines
- → Use of dominant language when appropriate
- → Study guides
- → Frontloading vocabulary (avoid jargon)
- → Thinking aloud
- → Visual & audio use of target language
- → Modeling and step by step instructions
- → Demonstrating
- → Multimedia
- → Gestures
- → Collaboration
- → Manipulatives
- → Hands on activities

When setting up groups for cooperative learning, be sure to remember:

- *Groups should be made intentionally, not randomly.*
    - *Some groups may include students who are similar levels (academically, language proficiency), while others are a mix of levels.*
    - *Other ways to create groups include interests, strengths in certain skills, and social/interactive opportunities.*
- *Groups should be dynamic, not static.*
- *Groups should change to allow students to meet the goals of the activity.*
- *Students should be required to take on different roles within groups. These roles should be tailored to the strengths of the members of the groups.*

- Teachers should keep content and language objectives in mind when planning activities and creating groups.

Establishing norms for collaborative group learning:

- All students must respect the contributions of everyone.
- All students must contribute in some fashion.
- All students support one another.
- All students must stay on task.
- All students must help and encourage one another. **Stay positive!**

Why should MLs work in collaborative groups?

- Allows MLs to practice speaking and listening in the target language without all eyes in the class on them
- Provides MLs the opportunity to interact with students who may be unfamiliar to them (and the chance for native-English speakers to do the same!)
- Allows all students to work in a variety of parts of the room
- Allows the teacher to differentiate assignments based on groups (or roles of students within groups)

Four domains of language learning and tips

Listening: Speak clearly and slowly (but not like a robot!) and provide MLs with rich language from which they can build their vocabulary. This means that the words you speak are not too difficult nor too easy for your students to learn and understand. You can pair this oral language with visuals, motions, or anything that helps your students understand. Providing key words in writing as well can help students understand the sounds of the words as they learn them.

Speaking: Provide varied opportunities for your MLs to speak (especially through collaborative learning). Be strategic with your groups and change often. Give the opportunity to prepare beforehand when MLs are asked to speak. Be cautious with correcting students when speaking--it takes a lot of bravery to speak in the target language and we don't want to discourage them!

Reading and **Writing**: Our MLs may not read and write at the same level as their native-English peers. Both language input and output may be differentiated for MLs. (Leveled readers, readers in native language, graphic organizers, output in a mixture of languages) Their literacy in their dominant language is valuable and can help them build their literacy in English.

ABOUT THE AUTHOR

Dr. Denise Furlong currently is working her dream job as a teacher educator for Georgian Court University in New Jersey. She has over 20 years experience teaching diverse learners and coaching their teachers in grades K-12. She lives at the Jersey Shore with her husband Tim, her kids (Ryan, Joey & Sarah), and their two dogs. You can connect with her on Twitter at @denise_furlong.

EduMatch
PUBLISHING